CONTENTS

PART ONE

INTRODUCTION

HOW TO STUDY A NOVEL

Studying a novel on your own requires self-discipline and a carefully thought-out work plan in order to be effective.

- You will need to read the novel more than once. Start by reading it quickly for pleasure, then read it slowly and thoroughly.

- On your second reading make detailed notes on the plot, characters and themes of the novel. Further readings will generate new ideas and help you to memorise the details of the story.

- Some of the characters will develop as the plot unfolds. How do your responses towards them change during the course of the novel?

- Think about how the novel is narrated. From whose point of view are events described?

- A novel may or may not present events chronologically: the time-scheme may be a key to its structure and organisation.

- What part do the settings play in the novel?

- Are words, images or incidents repeated so as to give the work a pattern? Do such patterns help you to understand the novel's themes?

- Identify what styles of language are used in the novel.

- What is the effect of the novel's ending? Is the action completed and closed, or left incomplete and open?

- Does the novel present a moral and just world?

- Cite exact sources for all quotations, whether from the text itself or from critical commentaries. Wherever possible find your own examples from the novel to back up your opinions.

- Always express your ideas in your own words.

This York Note offers an introduction to *The Mayor of Casterbridge* and cannot substitute for close reading of the text and the study of secondary sources.

The Mayor of Casterbridge ranks among Hardy's greatest tragic novels, along with *The Return of the Native*, *Tess of the d'Urbervilles* and *Jude the Obscure*. It is one of his 'Novels of Character and Environment', which he saw as his most important works of fiction.

Critics have compared *The Mayor of Casterbridge* to Greek tragedy and Elizabethan and Jacobean drama (particularly *King Lear*). Its tragic hero, Michael Henchard, is a powerful figure, whose downfall is deeply moving. Hardy's portrayal of his Man of Character is justly considered one of the great achievements of nineteenth-century fiction. Henchard has been compared to other obsessive Victorian heroes: Emily Brontë's Heathcliff in *Wuthering Heights* and Louis Trevelyan, in Anthony Trollope's *He Knew He Was Right*. What makes Hardy's **protagonist** unique is his psychological complexity and the fact that, in spite of his perverse character, we sympathise with him. Impulsive, reckless, cruel, Henchard is also capable of selfless generosity; his determination carries all before him. Henchard is never less than compelling. His rivalry with the Scot Donald Farfrae lies at the heart of the novel, but his relationships with women, which contribute to his undoing, equally highlight his good and bad qualities.

In his greatest novels Hardy explored a number of themes and ideas that are thought to express his view of life. Hardy denied that he possessed any specific philosophy, but his work shows that he was preoccupied by the effects of heredity, the roles of Fate and Chance and man's relationship with Nature. His tragic novels suggest that Hardy became increasingly pessimistic as he grew older. In them we see man struggling to survive in a universe that seems indifferent to his existence. At times there also seem to be malicious supernatural forces at work in the lives of his characters.

Hardy's fiction reveals his great attachment to his native Dorset countryside and his enjoyment in relating its history and customs. His descriptions of Casterbridge, based on Dorchester, capture the imagination, for this agricultural town is a powerful character in its own right, not merely a backdrop to the human dramas that unfold in its streets and houses. Hardy's inclusion of dialect words and an urban chorus (again, reminiscent of Greek drama) add yet more power to the novel.

The Mayor of Casterbridge is one of Hardy's most densely plotted books: the action moves swiftly and events are repeated and echoed, all of them leading relentlessly to the death of the tragic hero. As the novel was published first as a serial, the need to work in dramatic incidents each week meant that Hardy produced a novel full of arresting images and incidents. His use of different narrative points of view ensures that the reader remains 'hooked'.

On one occasion, when Virginia Woolf travelled down to Dorset to visit Hardy, she took *The Mayor of Casterbridge* to read on the train; she told its author that she could not put the book down. Readers today share her high opinion of this text, which is less pessimistic than *Tess* or *Jude the Obscure*, but no less intense.

PART TWO

SUMMARIES & COMMENTARIES

Like many Victorian novels The Mayor of Casterbridge *was originally published in serial form. Hardy began writing it after his return to Dorchester in 1883. By 1885 it was completed, and then published in weekly parts in* The Graphic, *beginning in January 1886. The first English book form of the text appeared in May 1886. Hardy complained about the demands that serialisation made on him as an artist. He thought that preparing it for weekly publication had marred* The Mayor of Casterbridge *more than any of his other works for it had compelled him to include incidents that would keep the reader 'hooked', regardless of his conception of the novel as a whole. Hardy also objected to the – as he saw it – prudish tastes of the magazine publishers: young females would be outraged by anything of a morally dubious nature, they claimed. Hardy referred disparagingly to this conservatism as 'Grundyism'. He was forced to practise a form of self-censorship; for example, he was obliged to have Henchard marry Lucetta when he assumes Susan is dead. Later, when he revised the story for book publication, Hardy removed some superfluous episodes and restored the illicit ambiguity of the Henchard–Lucetta relationship. Further revisions were made when the novel was republished in the 1890s, including the restoration of actual Dorchester place names.*

This Note refers to the 1997 Penguin Classics text of The Mayor of Casterbridge, *which incorporates the changes Hardy made for the 1895–6 Wessex Novels edition.*

SYNOPSIS

Hardy's story begins in the 1820s. Michael Henchard, journeying on foot across Wessex, in search of work, gets drunk at a fair at Weydon-Priors and auctions his wife Susan. She is bought by a sailor – Richard Newson – who emigrates to Canada with her and her daughter, Elizabeth-Jane. Filled with remorse, Henchard vows not to touch alcohol again for a period of twenty-one years. He searches unsuccessfully for his wife for a number of months, and arrives in Casterbridge. Eighteen years later Susan returns to Wessex, accompanied by her eighteen-year-old daughter Elizabeth-Jane. She believes that Newson has drowned at sea and hopes that Michael will help her and Elizabeth-Jane in some way. At the Weydon-Priors Fair she learns that Henchard can be found at Casterbridge, where he is now a prosperous corn merchant and mayor. A Scotsman, Donald Farfrae, arrives in Casterbridge at the same time as the two women. Henchard has had some trouble with sprouting wheat and Farfrae offers him a method of making it usable. Henchard, immediately drawn to Farfrae, persuades him to stay on as his manager. Having observed him at the inn, Elizabeth-Jane also feels an immediate attraction towards Farfrae. The following morning her mother sends Elizabeth-Jane to Henchard's house to announce their arrival. She is ignorant of her mother's true relationship with him, believing him to be a distant relative. Henchard is moved by the girl he assumes is his daughter and sends a note to Susan, asking her for a secret rendezvous, There, it is agreed that Susan should stay on in Casterbridge, so that Henchard can woo and remarry her, thus making reparation for his previous misdemeanour.

Increasingly reliant on and fond of Farfrae, who instigates new and successful business methods, Henchard confides in him the particulars of the auction and his wife's return. He also reveals that he has had a liaison with a young Jersey woman (discreetly withholding her name), whom he had promised to marry, assuming that Susan was dead. Farfrae is asked to draft a letter breaking off the engagement. Following a rather businesslike but respectable courtship Henchard and Susan marry. Henchard grows very attached to Elizabeth-Jane and suggests that she should take his surname, but Susan dissuades her daughter from doing so. As a result of the improvement in her circumstances, Elizabeth-Jane blossoms. Her attraction to Farfrae continues to grow, and he seems to be attracted to her in return, following a meeting in a barn, set up by an anonymous note-sender.

After a clash over the treatment of a workman, Abel Whittle, Henchard's relationship with Farfrae deteriorates. He becomes jealous of his popularity and begins to view him as a rival. Henchard dismisses Farfrae, who establishes his own business. He also informs his rival that he must have nothing more to do with Elizabeth-Jane. Susan becomes ill.

Lucetta Le Sueur -the young Jersey woman – writes to Henchard, to say that she will be passing through Casterbridge to collect her compromising love letters. However, she does not come: her aunt has died, leaving her a fortune. She adopts her aunt's surname, Templeman. Susan dies, leaving a letter for Henchard to read on Elizabeth-Jane's wedding day. But Henchard opens it and discovers that the girl is not his, but Newson's daughter. His feelings for Elizabeth-Jane change from love to dislike and, to rid himself of her, he decides to promote a match between her and Farfrae.

Meanwhile Lucetta has moved to Casterbridge, and by chance meets the lonely Elizabeth-Jane. She asks the girl to live with her as a companion. Lucetta still hopes to marry Henchard, but he does not pursue her as ardently as she had hoped and her feelings towards him cool. Farfrae comes to visit Elizabeth-Jane at Lucetta's house, and falls in love with Lucetta, who is immediately attracted to him. Henchard determines to ruin Farfrae, hiring Jopp as manager to assist him. But the weather again foils Henchard's plans, his business falters, and he dismisses Jopp. There is a confrontation between Henchard and Lucetta, witnessed by Elizabeth-Jane: Henchard has overheard Lucetta discussing marriage with Farfrae and, incensed, wrings a promise of marriage from her.

Shortly after this Henchard, acting as magistrate, is hearing a case when the defendant reveals the story of the wife auction at Weydon-Priors. Henchard is publicly disgraced. Increasingly isolated and on the verge of bankruptcy he moves into lodgings with Jopp. Elizabeth-Jane, also increasingly isolated, moves into lodgings when Lucetta reveals that she has married Farfrae. When Henchard is forced to sell up, Farfrae buys his house and business, although he attempts a reconciliation with his former employer. Henchard takes up a position as hay-trusser with Farfrae, but when he hears that Farfrae is likely to be made mayor, his jealousy returns. The loss of Lucetta to his rival also rankles, and when his vow of sobriety finishes Henchard begins to drink heavily. To his chagrin, Farfrae does succeed him as mayor and the reversal of fortunes is complete.

Henchard has not returned Lucetta's letters, which are still locked up in his old safe, so she writes to him. He goes to collect them and, in a tantalising scene, reads extracts to Farfrae, without revealing the writer's name. Henchard unwisely asks Jopp to deliver the letters and they are passed round and read in a local inn. A skimmington ride is planned to shame Lucetta and Henchard.

At a visit by an important royal personage to Casterbridge, Henchard arrives drunk and is pushed out of sight by the new mayor. Seeking revenge for this slight he lures Farfrae to his barn, intending to fight and kill him, but, when he has Farfrae at his mercy, finds himself unable to kill him. He lets him leave. Lucetta observes the skimmington ride in which effigies of herself and Henchard are paraded on a donkey. She collapses. Henchard races after Farfrae to tell him that his wife is dangerously ill, but he is not believed. On returning home later that evening Farfrae discovers that Lucetta is close to death. She dies that night.

The lonely Henchard draws closer to Elizabeth-Jane, but his relationship with her is threatened when Newson reappears, seeking Susan and his daughter. Henchard lies, telling him that both women are dead. Newson leaves Casterbridge. Full of remorse Henchard considers suicide, but seeing the effigy of himself (from the skimmington ride) in the river, takes this as a sign that he is meant to live. There follows a short period of increased happiness for him with his stepdaughter, but Farfrae's renewed interest in Elizabeth-Jane and another appearance by Newson persuade him that he should leave Casterbridge before his lies are uncovered. He resumes his work as a hay-trusser.

Meanwhile Elizabeth-Jane is reunited with her real father and her wedding to Farfrae takes place. Shortly after the marriage she starts to wonder what has happened to Henchard and asks her husband to seek him out. Eventually Farfrae and Elizabeth-Jane discover that he has died in a ramshackle cottage, attended by Abel Whittle, who describes Henchard's final days. Henchard has left a will in which he asks that he should be forgotten. The novel closes with a description of Elizabeth-Jane, who has matured into a thoughtful, sober and well balanced young woman, who serves her community and her husband well.

DETAILED SUMMARIES & COMMENTARIES

CHAPTER 1   Michael Henchard sells his wife

Michael Henchard, accompanied by his wife Susan and baby daughter Elizabeth-Jane, journeys across Wessex towards Weydon-Priors, hoping to find employment as a hay-trusser. Arriving at the village they discover a fair in progress. Michael buys furmity (a non-alcoholic drink) laced with rum. As he becomes drunk he bewails the fact that he is being held back because he has married too young. Increasingly belligerent, Henchard decides to sell Susan to the highest bidder. At first the spectators think that the auction is good sport, but it appears that the young man is serious. He raises his wife's price to five guineas and Susan is bought by a sailor, Richard Newson. Susan bitterly throws her wedding ring at Henchard, indicating that she accepts her sale as a legal contract. Henchard, who shows no remorse, spends the night sleeping in the furmity tent.

> Hardy carefully locates his story in time and place in this opening chapter, which, with the second chapter, serves as a **prologue**. The wife sale is a catalyst; a sensational – some would say **melodramatic** – event that has far-reaching consequences. It is here that the seeds of conflict are sown.
>
> The opening visual image of man moving across a landscape is typical of Hardy's almost cinematic technique: he gradually focuses in on his subjects after establishing them in a setting. His 'bird's eye' view of locations is repeated later, for example, when Susan and Elizabeth-Jane approach Casterbridge (Chapter 3). The setting suggests decline and weariness: the road is dusty, the young family on the move in search of work. Country life is thus made to seem precarious. The melancholy tone increases, for the central characters do not form a happy unit: the man ignores his wife and daughter and Susan, we are told, has the 'hard, half-apathetic expression of one who deems anything possible at the hands of Time and Chance, except, perhaps, fair-play' (p. 4). Much has been made of the roles of fate and chance in Hardy's novels, and many critics suggest that his work is essentially pessimistic. Hardy appears to present a negative view of marriage here, although we are most likely to feel critical not of the institution but of

the young husband, whose actions are described as 'an indefensible proceeding' (p. 15).

Hardy offers here an intriguing and precise portrait of Henchard – whose name we do not yet know; we will judge his future actions in the light of what we learn of him now. Hardy's descriptions are telling: this man may look shabby but he is also 'of fine figure, swarthy and stern in aspect' (p. 3). He possesses a 'dogged and cynical indifference' (p. 3) and 'the instinct of a perverse character' (p. 8). When drunk there is a 'fiery spark' in his dark eye and he becomes 'overbearing – even brilliantly quarrelsome' (p. 8). At this point he is not an attractive man; one of Hardy's achievements in this novel is to make us sympathise with a character who displays a large number of negative traits.

In contrast to the belligerent husband, Newson, whose sudden appearance suggests that chance already plays a role in the plot, appears to be kindly. When Susan goes with him, although social codes are being transgressed, we will probably feel that she and her daughter will have a better chance of happiness in the future, especially since her stock of marital happiness with Henchard has clearly never been great (he has threatened to sell her before). Hardy's method of introducing Newson is also typical of his technique: the sailor's voice is heard from the doorway of the tent; he has been listening unobserved. Eavesdropping and overheard conversations play a crucial role in this story. Other details prepare the reader for the breakdown of the Henchard marriage; the characters and setting at Weydon-Priors fair are unpromising, leading to a feeling of tension; the furmity woman is described as 'a haggish creature' who sells 'antiquated slop' (p. 7); before the wife sale there is a sale of the 'few inferior animals' remaining (p. 5); the fair is described as containing 'peep-shows, toy-stands, wax-works, inspired monsters...' (p. 7). By the time Henchard gets drunk the company in the furmity tent has 'decidedly degenerated' (p. 10). Hardy's effective, brief character sketches of the repugnant inhabitants of the tent help prepare us for what occurs.

The wife sale itself is shocking and we share Susan's anxiety, but this inhuman custom is clearly not unknown in rural Wessex; people are willing to participate so long as they think they are engaged in sport. This kind of ritual public humiliation – presented as entertainment – later proves fatal to Lucetta when the Casterbridge townsfolk put on a skimmity-ride. The gossip that occurs in the furmity tent will play an important role, and both men and women are its victims. In this opening chapter it also becomes apparent that social ambition and money are important: Henchard sells his wife and baby partly because he believes that they are holding him back. People are linked directly to property; Henchard is referred to as Susan's 'owner' (p. 11) and his rage when he finds that she has gone is proprietorial (in all his relationships Henchard behaves as if he owns those he loves). At the end of the chapter Henchard is left alone; for much of the novel he will seem to be an isolated figure.

fustian coarse cotton material

hay-trussing the cutting and securing of hay into bundles

furmity drink made from wheat, raisins, spices and milk

Maelstrom depths reference to the Greek myth of Scylla and Charybdis

the great trumpet reference to the Day of Judgement

CHAPTER 2   **Henchard searches fruitlessly for Susan and makes a vow of temperance**

Henchard wakes ashamed and regretful as he recalls the events of the previous evening, but he is also angry with Susan for leaving him. He resolves to search for his family. Coming across a church Henchard enters it and swears on oath not to touch alcohol for twenty-one years. After searching doggedly for a number of months he abandons his quest when he learns that Newson has emigrated to Canada. He journeys south-west and arrives in Casterbridge.

This chapter opens with the solitary Henchard surveying the landscape around him; as in the first chapter, man is contrasted with nature. There is a sense of a new beginning, established by the descriptions of the 'freshness of the September morning' and the 'newly risen sun' (p. 16), although Henchard is also preoccupied by the events of the night before. His character is now further developed and there are some hints that he is not entirely bad. His dogged determination to find his wife goes in his favour, as does his vow of temperance. Henchard is a proud man whose reputation is clearly important to him; he feels 'a certain shyness of revealing his conduct' (p. 18), which renders his search ineffectual. This will be a pattern in the novel; after he has acted rashly Henchard tries to make amends, but his attempts at reparation are often unsuccessful.

Seven Sleepers reference to the story of Ephesus, found in the Koran, in which seven Christians took refuge in a cave to escape persecution. They fell asleep for 300 years
sacrarium the sanctuary, or place in front of the altar in a church
foot-pace the priest stands here to offer the sacrament

CHAPTER 3   Eighteen years later Susan and her daughter Elizabeth-Jane arrive at Weydon-Priors, seeking Henchard

Susan, now calling herself 'Mrs Newson', walks towards Weydon-Priors with Elizabeth-Jane. Both women are dressed in black, mourning Newson, who is presumed to have drowned at sea. They are seeking their 'relation' Michael Henchard. Elizabeth-Jane has not been informed of her mother's previous relationship with Henchard. At the fair, Susan meets the furmity woman who tells her that Henchard can be found at Casterbridge.

The repeated journey on foot, with mother and daughter hand in hand, contrasts sharply with Susan's previous fateful, silent walk to Weydon-Priors. The closeness of the women is further established by their dialogue, which enables Hardy to convey both emotions and information, while the passage of time is revealed by descriptions of characters and settings. The fair is the victim of economic decline; now the furmity woman struggles to make a living. There is irony in the fact that she does not recall Susan, whose life was changed so radically by the events of a previous fair. Like Henchard, Susan has kept her actions secret. She also shares some of her first husband's determination. Hardy now begins to develop the women's characters: Elizabeth-Jane's desire for respectability – a key feature of her characterisation – is apparent in her reaction to the furmity woman, who will make two further significant appearances. Deception becomes an important theme. Both Elizabeth-Jane and the reader remain ignorant of the girl's true paternity, although Susan's unease at Elizabeth-Jane's questions hints at the truth.

withy willow
soi-disant so-called

CHAPTER 4   **Arriving in Casterbridge, Susan and Elizabeth-Jane overhear an argument about Henchard**

We learn that, clearly, Susan accepted her purchase by the sailor as binding. After twelve years in Canada the family returned to England and set up home in Falmouth, Cornwall. Confiding in a friend, Susan was horrified to learn that her 'marriage' was not legal. Thus, when the sailor was reported lost at sea, she was almost relieved. Knowing that her daughter wishes to better herself, Susan hopes that she can find a way out of their straitened circumstances by contacting Henchard and asking for his assistance. But, fearing Elizabeth-Jane's reaction, she has not disclosed her history with Henchard.

The two women hear an argument which confirms that Henchard is a resident of Casterbridge and that he evokes mixed responses in the town's inhabitants. People are complaining about the shortage of edible bread, which is a result of the corn-factor (Henchard) selling bad wheat.

A **flashback** is used to give us further information about Susan's past. Her desire to improve Elizabeth-Jane's prospects makes us sympathise with her, as does her weariness of life and the fact that her 'health was not what it once had been' (p. 27); Hardy is **foreshadowing** her decline and death here. We understand that Elizabeth-Jane has potential and we see Casterbridge for the first time through her eyes. Hardy delineates the town carefully, offering detailed, concrete descriptions of sights and sounds; this is part of his **realism**. He is interested in architecture and the past, shown by his inclusion of the Roman history of Casterbridge. Although the women have arrived in an urban community, there is a strong sense that agriculture and rural life are important. As in earlier chapters, dialect is used to add colour. The chapter ends on a tense note: all is not well because of the spoiled wheat. Hardy deliberately withholds information about Henchard's position.

brick-nogging bricks between timber frames
seed-lips seed baskets
Sicilian Mariners' Hymn a traditional tune, which provided the setting for a number of nineteenth-century hymns
swipes weak beer
corn-factor a merchant who buys and sells corn
grown wheat sprouting wheat that cannot be used successfully in baking

CHAPTER 5   **Henchard, now mayor of Casterbridge, presides over a banquet at The Golden Crown. Susan and Elizabeth-Jane hear him discussed by townsfolk**

A crowd has gathered outside The Golden Crown and people observe the lavish dinner through the open window. Hearing that Henchard is now an important and successful businessman, as well as mayor, Susan feels less sure about approaching him, although Elizabeth-Jane is pleased to think that her 'relation' is a prosperous and significant personage. Henchard is now a teetotaller, and understood to be a widower. He is currently embroiled in professional difficulties due to the sale of bad wheat: a citizen challenges him. Henchard does not like the interruption or the slur against his reputation, but admits the errors he has made and says that he is advertising for a manager to prevent future mistakes in his corn business.

Henchard's reappearance is dramatic; the contrast between the dusty hay-trusser and the well-dressed mayor is stark. We observe him through the women's eyes, framed by a window. In spite of his rise in society it is clear that Henchard's temper is still uncertain, that his sophisticated and impressive exterior barely conceals his passionate and impulsive core: he has to work hard at restraint. Henchard remains isolated, signified by his temperance. We can sympathise with Susan when she says 'he overpowers me' (p. 33);

although the mayor's authority is challenged when the citizen complains about the bread through the window. In succeeding chapters Henchard is challenged many times. Here he appears to be in control, however; he answers the charges laid against him and is ready to admit his mistakes. Hardy sets up suspense: what will happen when Henchard's vow of temperance is completed? How will the introduction of a manager affect his business? How will he react when he meets Susan and Elizabeth-Jane? Time is also used to maintain tension; we are told that nineteen years have passed since the auction, and yet Elizabeth-Jane is only eighteen. The use of rural 'types' to comment on Henchard's progress and character further points to the significance of gossip and reputation.

'The Roast Beef of Old England' a popular song, taken from *The Grub Street Opera* (1731)

portico entrance

fall veil

rummers large glasses without stems

banded teetotaller someone who is a member of a temperance band

jovial Jews a reference to Exodus 32 and the Israelites, who worshipped the golden calf, thereby incurring God's wrath

CHAPTER 6   **Farfrae despatches a note to Henchard, offering to assist him in the matter of the substandard wheat**

Donald Farfrae, a young Scotsman passing through Casterbridge, overhears the conversation in The Golden Crown and asks a waiter to deliver a note to Henchard. He also asks him to recommend a cheaper hotel where he can find lodgings. The King of Prussia is recommended and he immediately proceeds there. Elizabeth-Jane suggests to her mother that they should follow Farfrae's example, since he seems respectable, and the women also repair to the inn. When he receives Farfrae's note Henchard is immediately intrigued and sets out to find the Scotsman.

Another stranger arrives by chance; like Newson, Farfrae will have an enormous impact on Henchard's life. The Scot is described in positive terms as a young man of 'remarkably pleasant aspect'

(p. 37); he contrasts vividly with Henchard physically, but shares some of his future employer's impulsiveness. He is also compared to the Biblical figure David, a reference that hints at events to come. Elizabeth-Jane's interest in Farfrae is established immediately; again we observe a character through her eyes; for much of the novel the girl is cast in the role of onlooker and we come to trust her judgement. Social distinctions are drawn out in the description of the King of Prussia.

fair and ruddy echoes descriptions of David (1 Samuel 16:12 and 17:42)

yard of clay a long clay pipe

CHAPTER 7   Susan and Elizabeth-Jane overhear Henchard's conversation with Farfrae

Elizabeth-Jane offers to work at the inn, and is called on to take up Farfrae's supper. She is clearly drawn to him. The two women are staying in a room adjoining Farfrae's, and can hear the conversation that is taking place next door. Henchard has called on Farfrae. The latter describes and demonstrates a method for reclaiming spoiled corn. Impressed by the young man, Henchard presses him to accept the position of manager, but the Scot is intent on emigrating to America.

The differences between Henchard and Farfrae are developed here: through the discussion about the corn Henchard is associated with clumsy destruction, Farfrae with amelioration. Henchard's impulsiveness is shown by his willingness to disregard Jopp's prior claim in order to offer a job to a man he does not know. There is irony here too; nineteen years before Henchard gave his worldly goods away (Susan and his daughter); now he prepares to place his business in a stranger's hands. We might feel that Henchard is a sentimentalist: he is drawn to Farfrae partly because the young man resembles his dead brother. His loneliness makes us sympathise with him and we can see that there are irreconcilable impulses in Henchard; he craves affection but is ill at ease in close personal relationships; has devoted his life to business success and the establishment of his reputation, but remains personally unfulfilled. We might also feel sympathy for Henchard because it is clear that he cannot escape the past: the sale of his wife haunts him still, as we learn when he tells Farfrae that he has committed actions he is ashamed of. Hardy makes excellent use of one of his favourite narrative techniques in this chapter; Susan and Elizabeth-Jane eavesdrop on the conversation between the two men through the partition, with the latter's constant apprehension increasing tension for the reader. Another Hardyan device, the missed opportunity, occurs when Elizabeth-Jane serves Farfrae his supper and he fails to look up at her. In this chapter the girl shows that she is self-sacrificing and hard-working, earning our respect.

twelve-bushel strength the quantity of barley used when brewing; the implication here is that The King of Prussia sells strong ale
Presbyterian cream cream laced with whisky
the dog days a reference to the hottest days of the year, when the Dog Star is in the ascendancy

CHAPTER 8   **Farfrae joins the crowd downstairs in The King of Prussia**

When Henchard leaves, Farfrae makes his way to the public rooms downstairs. He talks to some of the drinkers who frequent the inn and sings some Scottish ballads, impressing everyone with his skill. Having cleared away his supper tray, Elizabeth discreetly watches Farfrae too. When he returns upstairs to go to bed he passes her on the stairs and sings her a ditty. She is too embarrassed to look at him, although she talks to her mother about him. Henchard cuts a rather sad figure as he listens to the singing from the street, pacing up and down alone.

This chapter does not advance the plot a great deal, but provides us with another view of Casterbridge life. The drinking and singing in The King of Prussia contrast sharply with the formal, lavish banquet at The Golden Crown. The vitality of the townsfolk is entertaining, although there is an unsavoury, brutal element too, which will become important later. Elizabeth-Jane remains a quiet observer; we see that she and Farfrae would be well-matched since she is of sober character and admires 'the serious light' in which the Scot 'looked at serious things' (pp. 54–5). Farfrae charms everyone with his affable manner; unlike Henchard he mixes easily. He is clearly able to dominate gatherings; we might feel that this could be a future source of conflict between mayor and manager. The central characters are drawn together here; all four are mentioned in the final paragraphs of this chapter, although Hardy is most concerned with Henchard, who evokes sympathy when he describes his loneliness and assumes the role of onlooker outside the inn.

lammigers (dialect) lame people
Gallows Hill a reference to an incident in the English Civil War, when 300 people were sentenced to death
bruckle (dialect) rough or untrustworthy
Botany Bay an area housing a penal colony for transported criminals in Australia
'Oh Nannie' an English song that was popular in Scotland
chine the rim of a beer barrel
Arthur's Seat a hill near Edinburgh. Legend has it King Arthur watched the defeat of the Picts from this hill

CHAPTER 9   Farfrae accepts Henchard's offer of work. Susan sends Elizabeth-Jane to Henchard with a note

The following morning Henchard accompanies Farfrae as he makes his way towards the Bristol Road, and urges him to stay on in Casterbridge as his manager. Meanwhile Elizabeth-Jane is sent to Henchard with a note, announcing Susan's arrival and requesting a meeting. In spite of this note Susan is quite prepared to leave Casterbridge at once if her husband does not wish to see her. When Elizabeth-Jane arrives at Henchard's office she is taken aback to find Donald Farfrae installed and busy working. Again he seems not to recognise her. In a **flashback** we discover how Farfrae was finally persuaded to stay on.

This chapter is carefully constructed to show the lives of the main characters becoming intertwined against the Casterbridge backdrop. Business and personal interests are linked through the movements and meetings of the characters, notably when Henchard declares to Farfrae, 'Now you are my friend!' (p. 63) when the Scot accepts the post of manager. We get a view of the bustling market day as Elizabeth-Jane makes her way to Henchard's house; we are reminded of the importance of agricultural life to the town. Henchard's prosperity is emphasised. Farfrae and Elizabeth-Jane are linked again when the girl finds the new manager in Henchard's office. Hardy deliberately uses this meeting – and the prior meeting between Henchard and Farfrae – to delay the encounter between Elizabeth-Jane and Henchard, building up suspense.

chassez-déchassez   a French dance in which the dancers step from right to left

Terpsichorean   the Greek Muse of dancing

'bloody warriors'   wallflowers

Cranstoun's Goblin Page   a reference to Scott's poem, 'The Lay of the Last Minstrel', in which Lord Cranstoun's malicious dwarf interrupts his master's wedding festivities with a cruel practical joke

staddles   large stone mushrooms used to raise the floor off the ground

CHAPTER 10   **Henchard welcomes Elizabeth-Jane and agrees to a meeting with Susan**

As Elizabeth-Jane waits for Henchard Joshua Jopp – who applied for and expected to secure the job that Farfrae has now taken – arrives. Henchard brusquely dismisses him. Elizabeth-Jane introduces herself as Susan Newson's daughter. Henchard immediately realises that his wife has kept the truth from her, but is pleased to see the girl he assumes is his daughter. He writes a note to Susan and encloses five guineas with it, effectively buying his wife back. This is a gesture of remorse and reparation. Henchard momentarily wonders whether the women are impostors, but just as swiftly rejects this thought, reassured by the girl's demeanour. Susan finds that she is expected to meet Henchard at the Ring on the Budmouth Road.

Hardy focuses on Henchard's emotions and others' reactions to him. The abrupt handling of Jopp contrasts with Henchard's 'wooing' of Farfrae; while the latter continues to gain friends, the mayor has now made an enemy, which proves significant later. However, his interaction with Elizabeth-Jane shows that Henchard is capable of greater sensitivity and tact. He is genuinely moved by the appearance of the girl. Even here business and the personal are linked: the contrite note to Susan is accompanied by money. Henchard's momentary concern that Elizabeth-Jane is an impostor is **ironic**: the future will show that she is not whom she seems to be. In this chapter the past begins to catch up with Henchard; in spite of his assertive behaviour we start to feel that the mayor might be overwhelmed. There is a hint that his relationship with Farfrae may not proceed smoothly; although Henchard is – so far – able to dominate his manager, Farfrae is described as 'a beginner *in charge*' (p. 65) (my emphasis).

the quicker cripple at Bethesda Jesus cured a man who had been unable to get into a pool at Bethesda in Jerusalem, said to have healing properties (John 5: 2–9)

Pembroke tables elegant eighteenth-century tables

a 'Josephus' The *Life* of Josephus (AD37–95), a Jewish historian and soldier

'Whole Duty of Man' an anonymous book of devotions of 1658, commonly found in respectable households during this period

Chippendale and Sheraton eighteenth-century English furniture designers

CHAPTER 11   Henchard and Susan agree to remarry, after a respectable period of courtship

The Ring is situated in the remains of a Roman Amphitheatre on the outskirts of Casterbridge. It is a gloomy and forbidding location, frequently used for clandestine meetings. Husband and wife meet here in the evening. Susan concurs with Henchard's plan that she and Elizabeth-Jane rent a cottage in the town, paid for by him, so that he can court and remarry his wife. He is anxious that their previous relationship should remain concealed from Elizabeth-Jane, who will become his stepdaughter in the eyes of the world.

As in the opening chapter, a setting is used to establish and reflect the moods of the characters. Hardy shows his own personal interest in the grotesque and macabre when he describes the Ring. The atmosphere of fear and superstition that prevails in the amphitheatre is entirely appropriate to Susan and Henchard's relationship. The description of the history of this location introduces a cosmic perspective and **foreshadows** events to come. The Ring has been the scene of public spectacle and violence; later Henchard will be brought down in a humiliatingly public manner. Henchard's reunion with Susan is uneasy. There is little love shown: Susan's self-sacrifice is emphasised, while Henchard is anxious about maintaining secrecy so that his reputation is unsullied.

Jötuns giants from Scandinavian folklore

Hadrian's soldiery the Emperor Hadrian (AD76–138) was responsible for the construction of the wall named after him

Aeolian modulations from Shelley's 'Prometheus Unbound', IV, 188. Aeolus was the Greek god of the winds

there's the rub o't very similar to Hamlet's phrase, 'ay there's the rub' from his famous soliloquy in III.1, in which he considers suicide

CHAPTER 12   Henchard confides his past history in Farfrae

When he returns Henchard discovers that Farfrae is still at work, attempting to organise the bookkeeping. The two men share a meal at Henchard's home and the mayor discloses his past to his new friend as they sit by the fire. This includes his marriage to and auction of Susan and a liaison with a young woman from Jersey, who nursed him during an illness. He has promised to marry this woman, whose reputation suffered as a result of her relationship with Henchard. Now that his wife has returned Henchard is determined to act honourably; he decides that he must send a letter of apology to the Jersey woman, breaking off his engagement. Henchard asks Farfrae to draft the letter for him. A cheque is enclosed with it. In spite of being urged by Farfrae to reveal the truth to Elizabeth-Jane, Henchard remains adamant that she must not learn of his and her mother's past conduct. He goes out to post his letter.

Henchard's and Farfrae's business methods are contrasted. Henchard continues to act impulsively when he confides in Farfrae; his confidences about the young Jersey woman introduce an intriguing new plot complication and further establish his ineptitude in personal affairs; again Henchard hopes to 'buy' a female's obedience with 'a useful sum of money' (p. 78). **Ironically**, Henchard declares that he is 'something of a woman-hater' (p. 76), and yet he has formed another troublesome liaison. We are forced to conclude that he has an overwhelming – and uncontrollable – urge for human affection and suspect that this new piece of his past will also catch up with Henchard. Interestingly, the young Jersey woman's family background seems to be rather unfortunate and not entirely respectable; is this to be significant in her character development later on? The introduction of this character also suggests that there is little chance of the reunion between Henchard and Susan providing happiness to either party.

Achilles the Greek hero, educated by Chiron in sporting and military pursuits

espaliers fruit trees grown horizontally

leafy Laocoons Laocoon, the Trojan priest of Apollo, was crushed to death by serpents

Job Job's curse, 'Let the day perish wherein I was born ...' (Job 3:3)

CHAPTER 13   Henchard and Susan remarry

Elizabeth-Jane and her mother are established in their cottage. Henchard provides them with a servant. He visits regularly, 'courting' Susan and the couple marry after two months. It becomes apparent that Henchard is acting out of a sense of duty. Nor does Susan appear to be particularly at ease. The match puzzles the townsfolk, who feel that Susan is beneath the mayor socially, and not possessed of many personal attractions. Observing the wedding they relate anecdotes of other much livelier marriages.

The melancholy westerly prospect of the cottage she moves into with Elizabeth-Jane suits Susan, who seems increasingly fragile. It is **ironic** that Henchard believes Elizabeth-Jane is being hoodwinked: he, future chapters will reveal, is the one labouring under illusions about his 'daughter'. Given his reaction to her in future chapters, there is irony too in the fact that he feels drawn to her. Hardy makes use of his chorus of townsfolk again: their easy joviality contrasts with the awkwardness of the Henchard–Susan union, although comments about the mayor's 'bluebeardy' (p. 83) look suggest that trouble is brewing. The anecdotes about marriage add to the sense of unease in this chapter. Social distinctions and gossip continue to play an important role.

the flesh is weak Christ's admonition to his disciples in the garden of Gethsemane (Matthew 26:41)

cow-barton cow shed

twanking (dialect) complaining, whining

CHAPTER 14   Elizabeth-Jane and Farfrae are brought together by an anonymous note-sender

Susan and Elizabeth-Jane find life at Henchard's home comfortable; Elizabeth-Jane enjoys her new-found prosperity. But she behaves prudently and does not spend lavishly on clothes. She gradually emerges as a beauty, although Casterbridge is slow to appreciate her charms. Henchard grows more and more attached to Elizabeth-Jane and hopes she will adopt his surname, but his desire is thwarted by his wife, who persuades the girl that this would be disloyal to Newson. The matter is dropped. Henchard has also become very fond of and reliant on Farfrae, although it is becoming increasingly apparent that the two men have very different temperaments. Farfrae's new business methods prove extremely successful. Elizabeth-Jane and Farfrae are tricked into an unexpected rendezvous at Dummerford granary.

Elizabeth-Jane's blossoming coincides with her mother's decline. The description of her world view early in the chapter foreshadows the final paragraphs of the novel. Her calm temperament contrasts with Henchard's more volatile nature. Farfrae is increasingly drawn to the girl and his courteous treatment of Elizabeth-Jane contrasts with Henchard's more awkward behaviour. The mayor's 'tigerish affection' (p. 88) for his manager now seems too possessive and consuming, although he is dismissive of the younger man's physical attributes. Farfrae's lesser strength becomes significant in Chapter 38. The narrator begins to prepare the reader for the revelation of Elizabeth-Jane's paternity: Henchard notes that the girl's hair is light brown rather than black and Susan is not keen that her daughter take his surname. The chapter ends on a more relaxed note than is usual in this novel, with Donald and Elizabeth-Jane enjoying their meeting after an awkward beginning. Their mutual attraction is shown in the rather erotic scene in which he blows the chaff out of her hair.

Martinmas summer the feast of St Martin was held on 11 November, during the 'Indian summer'

puffings elaborate clothes with puffed sleeves and frills

coulter the cutter at the front of a plough

spencer close-fitting bodice

winnowing machine used to separate grain from chaff

victorine a fur tippet fastened at the front, with the two ends hanging down

CHAPTER 15   **Henchard and Farfrae clash over the treatment of Abel Whittle**

Gradually Elizabeth-Jane is recognised as the town beauty; Farfrae becomes more interested in her as time passes. She, meanwhile, is preoccupied with improving herself intellectually. The good relationship between the mayor and his manager is threatened when Henchard humiliates an employee who is persistently late for work. Abel Whittle is hauled out of bed one morning by an irate Henchard, who forces him to report for duty without his breeches. Farfrae overrides his master and tells Whittle to return home and get dressed. When Henchard hears of this he quarrels with Farfrae in front of the men. He is further piqued when a small boy reveals that Farfrae is becoming more popular and trusted than he is.

> Elizabeth-Jane's attitude towards her own beauty contrasts with Lucetta's vanity later in the novel. As Elizabeth-Jane and Farfrae grow closer to one another, Henchard's relationship with the Scot deteriorates, especially after their clash over Whittle. This incident is by turns comic and distressing. Ultimately we shall share Farfrae's dim view of Henchard's actions. It is **ironic** that Abel declares he 'can't outlive the disgrace' (p. 97); later, alone and degraded, Henchard will be succoured by the man he treats so cruelly here. Henchard is personally and publicly 'hurt' (p. 98) by

his disagreement with Donald, and it is his perception of his waning public popularity that leads him to a feel a 'dim dread' of his manager (p. 100). It is particularly poignant that a child informs him that he is no longer the most admired man in Casterbridge. Again Henchard finds himself regretting his impulsive actions, and fearing the revelation of his secrets.

Baruch a spokesman for the prophet Jeremiah

Rochefoucauld French philosopher (1613–80), who suggested that self-love was the motivating force in human behaviour

scantling a scrap or small piece

chap o' wax a successful man whose fortunes are improving

sotto voce (Italian) in a low voice, under one's breath

CHAPTER 16   Henchard dismisses Farfrae

Henchard and Farfrae are at odds again, although the latter is unaware of the developing jealousy and antagonism his employer feels towards him. Both men organise festivities for a national holiday; Henchard is determined to outshine Farfrae. However, his outdoor celebrations are ruined by rain, while Farfrae's dance in a makeshift tent goes off successfully, with Susan and Elizabeth-Jane in attendance. When townsmen comment that Henchard has been bested the mayor announces – in Donald's presence – that the Scotsman will not remain in his service much longer. The following day Henchard bitterly regrets his impulsive remarks, but Farfrae has taken him at his word.

This chapter focuses on Henchard's relationship with Farfrae; it is a struggle for the mayor to behave in a formal and distant manner, but he cannot tolerate the loss of social standing that he is experiencing. His plans for the festivities reflect his nature: he wishes to make a grand gesture and believes that spending money will help him succeed, but Henchard does not plan ahead. However, his decision to distribute the food is a characteristically generous move. The change in Henchard's fortunes is signalled by the change in the weather: this is a key chapter for the mayor. The newcomer's novel ideas lead to a social triumph; it also appears that Farfrae is a desirable partner, popular with women, highlighting the different perceptions people have of the young Scot and his master. When he is 'challenged' by Farfrae's popularity Henchard's reaction is typically swift – and brutal. His dismissal of Farfrae leads to isolation and his character seems to control his fate at this point. The chapter closes with the impetuous Henchard's sense of regret. In contrast to Henchard, Farfrae displays a quiet dignity.

Correggio (1494–1534) famous Italian painter

stunpoll foolish fellow

'Miss McLeod of Ayr' an old Scottish tune, much loved by Hardy

randy merry-making

Jack's as good as his master (proverb) the servant has become as good as his employer

CHAPTER 17   **Farfrae sets up in business himself**

Farfrae accompanies Elizabeth-Jane home after the dance and hints that he would like to propose to her. She asks Farfrae not to leave Casterbridge now that he has broken with her stepfather and continues to be absorbed by thoughts of him. The Scot buys his own hay and corn business and prospers, although he initially refuses to compete with Henchard, who maligns him to the town council and forbids Elizabeth-Jane to see him. He also writes to Farfrae telling him to stay away from the girl. The two corn merchants become commercial rivals, and Henchard's bitterness grows when Farfrae is offered a stall at Casterbridge market.

It is **ironic** that Farfrae is on the verge of proposing to Elizabeth-Jane at the very moment that he breaks with Henchard; it is also sadly ironic that the girl should now – when it is too late – give in to her fantasies about Donald. The language used to describe the 'tussle' (p. 110) between Farfrae and Henchard reflects the latter's strength of feeling: the two become engaged in a 'war of prices' (p. 113) during their 'mortal commercial combat' (p. 113). However, Farfrae is a reluctant adversary. The narrator stresses that the mayor is personally wounded by the break with Farfrae: he sounds like a distressed child or distraught lover in the description (p. 110). He is also compared to Faust and Bellerophon, a character from Greek legend who killed his brother and fled from society. There is authorial intervention of a very direct kind when Hardy says, 'Character is Fate, said Novalis ...' (p. 112). Some critics suggest that this view contradicts Hardy's use of chance and other impersonal forces to direct his characters' lives. However, at this point in *The Mayor of Casterbridge* it seems clear that the 'same unruly volcanic stuff beneath the rind' (p. 110) that led Henchard to behave impetuously in his youth is controlling his destiny here. His 'amazing energy' (p. 111) brought him success, but now we learn that his temperament has prevented him from making friends. We are not surprised at his increasing isolation, which is a direct result of his uncompromising attitude, as shown in his instructions to Elizabeth-Jane regarding Donald, 'He is an enemy to our house' (p. 111). Meanwhile, Farfrae is quietly integrated into the business community.

varden farthing

modus vivendi (Latin) way of living, living arrangements

Like Jacob in Padan-Aram Jacob was tricked into marrying his cousin Leah by his uncle Laban, for whom he worked for seven years in order to earn Leah's sister Rachel's hand. Eventually Jacob became more prosperous than his uncle. See Genesis 30:25–43

Novalis the pen-name of Baron Friedrich von Hardenburg, Frederick Leopold (1772–1801), the German Romantic poet. Hardy probably used Eliot's *Mill on the Floss* (1860) as a source

Faust the source is probably Carlyle's essay 'Goethe's Helena', in which Faust is described as 'vehement and gloomy'. Faust sold his soul to the devil

dirk rapier

Bellerophon Greek hero who killed his brother, angering the gods. He ended his days as an outcast

CHAPTER 18   **Lucetta writes to Henchard from Jersey. Susan dies**

Henchard receives a letter from Lucetta, requesting the return of her love letters. She suggests a discreet meeting in Casterbridge when she passes through the town, so that she can collect the letters in person. When she does not appear Henchard returns home with the letters. Meanwhile

Susan has fallen ill. Henchard employs a rich, busy doctor to attend on her but she knows that death is near and writes a letter directed to her husband, which is to be opened on Elizabeth-Jane's wedding day. Elizabeth-Jane nurses her mother and learns that it was Susan who sent the anonymous notes which resulted in the meeting at Dummerford granary. Susan had hoped to promote a match between her daughter and Farfrae. We learn that Susan has died when Farfrae calls at Henchard's house one Sunday morning.

> Hardy focuses on Henchard's old and new 'loves', who are strikingly different. It is **ironic** that Lucetta should reappear and Henchard consider marrying her just as Susan is about to die. The women's letters – like all the letters and notes in this novel – are to prove highly significant: they will be opened and read at inappropriate times, leading to woe. Susan's death and Mother Cuxsom's epitaph for her are suitably poignant, there is a focus on her domestic qualities and superstition. It is also fitting that Susan's final wishes are only half fulfilled. In contrast, Lucetta's letter reveals a more lively character, who discloses her feelings freely, although she too has her secrets to keep. We notice that Lucetta is preoccupied by her appearance: she writes that she will be wearing her 'Paisley shawl with a red centre' (p. 115) when she passes through Casterbridge. Ironically, Henchard suspects her of 'a little *ruse*'; Susan's mysterious letter reveals a far greater ruse. The final paragraph contains a warning that Susan's secrets will all come out. Henchard's belief that he should marry Lucetta if he has the chance proves that he has a sense of justice.

ounce pennies privately minted coins used in trade
doxology theology

CHAPTER 19   **Elizabeth-Jane's paternity is revealed**

Three weeks after Susan's funeral Henchard decides to tell Elizabeth-Jane that he is her father. He explains that he separated from her mother and presents her relationship with Newson as a remarriage, which took place because he was assumed to be dead. Elizabeth-Jane is bewildered but concurs with Henchard's wish that she should now take his surname. A letter is despatched to the *Casterbridge Chronicle*. Searching for a document which proves his marriage to Susan, Henchard comes across his wife's letter, which is clumsily sealed. He opens it and discovers that Elizabeth-Jane is not his daughter; his baby Elizabeth-Jane died in infancy, three months after the auction. Utterly wretched, he spends the night walking through the gloomiest parts of Casterbridge and along by the riverbank. He decides to keep Susan's revelation to himself. The following morning at breakfast Henchard is greeted warmly by Elizabeth-Jane, who has accepted him as her true father.

This chapter contains a number of cruel **ironies**. At the moment that he draws closer to Elizabeth-Jane Henchard is unable to follow 'the policy of leaving well alone' (p. 119) and finds his hopes dashed by Susan's letter and its 'blasting disclosure' (p. 123). The composition of the letter to the *Casterbridge Chronicle* is also ironic: the public announcement that Elizabeth-Jane is to take his name coincides with Henchard's feeling that he cannot 'endure the sight' of the girl (p. 124). Finally, in another cruelly ironic blow, Elizabeth-Jane finally accepts Henchard as her father. Henchard is increasingly lonely and begins to feel that he is being punished: 'I am to suffer, I perceive' he says (p. 123). The cruelty of time and fate make the mayor 'unnerved and purposeless' (p. 123), and he gloomily concludes that his life is 'dust and ashes' (p. 126). Towards the end of the chapter he takes a solitary walk in a setting by the river that is entirely appropriate to his state of mind. This image of Henchard walking alone is a recurrent motif; eventually he will remove himself from Casterbridge and die in rural obscurity.

pier-glass mirror
the avowal of Joseph 'Joseph said unto his brethren, "I am Joseph; doth my father yet live?" And his brethren could not answer him: for they were troubled at his presence' (Genesis 45:3)
Prester John the mythical Christian ruler from the East who tried to make paradise part of his kingdom. He was punished and blinded by the gods
Schwarzwasser (German) black water

chapter 20   Henchard treats Elizabeth-Jane harshly. She meets a
stranger

Elizabeth-Jane works hard to improve herself but is continually criticised
by Henchard, who treats her coldly and harshly. She becomes isolated
and unhappy. Visiting her mother's grave she sees an attractive female
stranger, who has also visited the grave. Deciding that it might be a good
idea to have the girl taken off his hands, Henchard writes to Farfrae
telling him that he may court Elizabeth. He is disappointed and angry
when he learns that he has not been made an alderman, especially since
Farfrae has been invited to join the Town Council. When she meets the
stranger again Elizabeth-Jane is pleased to be offered the chance of a
new, more congenial home at High Street Hall: the lady has asked her to
be her companion-housekeeper.

> We feel great sympathy for Elizabeth-Jane – 'a dumb, deep-feeling,
> great-eyed creature' (p. 131) – as Hardy dwells on Henchard's 'open
> chiding' (p. 126) of her. Farfrae also ignores the humble girl,
> foreshadowing his treatment of Elizabeth-Jane later on. We pity
> Henchard too: he is as miserable as his victim. He is tortured by his
> extreme emotions, believing now that Farfrae is 'a treacherous
> upstart' (p. 133). Hardy sets up new feelings of suspense with the
> introduction of another charming stranger, who initially resembles
> Elizabeth-Jane, although the 'artistic perfection' (p. 132) of her
> appearance suggests she is not really the younger woman's 'wraith
> or double'. What are we to make of the stranger's curious 'anxiety
> not to condemn' (p. 135) Henchard when she talks with Elizabeth-
> Jane?

marks of the beast see Revelations 13:17
Minerva the Roman goddess of wisdom, she is also protectress of
commerce
Princess Ida from Tennyson's 'The Princess' (1847)
Austerlitz the Czech town where Napoleon won a great victory in 1805.
However, he lost the war against the Russian and Austrian armies
leery worn out or weak

CHAPTER 21   Elizabeth-Jane moves to High Street Hall

Elizabeth-Jane visits High Street Hall secretly at night and sees that her new acquaintance has already moved in. Not wishing to be seen she conceals herself in an alleyway when she hears footsteps. She does not notice that Henchard has entered the house by a rear door. When she returns home she asks Henchard if she might be allowed to leave him. He agrees to her request and offers Elizabeth-Jane a small allowance. She makes her arrangements to move out the next day, following another meeting with the lady – Miss Templeman. When he discovers her preparing to leave so soon Henchard regrets his harsh treatment of Elizabeth (entering her room he has seen the efforts towards self-improvement she has made) and tries to persuade her to stay. But it is too late. Henchard is further taken aback when he is informed of the girl's new address.

> The chapter opens with the current Casterbridge gossip about High Street Hall, which is to become an important location for all the characters. The description of the house is informed by Hardy's interest in architecture and our attention is drawn to the 'queer old door' that suggests 'intrigue' (p. 139). Henchard's indifference to Elizabeth-Jane leads him to offer her money: another example of the way he attempts to 'buy' those he feels a moral responsibility for. Ironically, he changes his mind and decides he would prefer Elizabeth to stay, but it is 'ten minutes too late' (p. 143). The narrator seems ambivalent about Lucetta; we are told that 'there might be some devilry about her presence' (p. 141) It also seems that Lucetta – like Susan – has resorted to cunning to achieve her aims.

passengers means passers-by here
Palladian an Italian architectural style
'tailing' bits of corn
fly a carriage

CHAPTER 22   Lucetta waits for Henchard to call on her

The chapter opens with another flashback, which informs us of the reason for Henchard's visit to High Street Hall in Chapter 21. He was responding to a letter from Lucetta, announcing her arrival in Casterbridge. He then receives a further note from Lucetta, in which she reveals that she has inherited a fortune and taken her dead aunt's name, Templeman. She wishes to conceal her past as Lucette Le Sueur. Lucetta seems to be keen that Henchard should marry her. He is not averse to the idea. However, when he makes his second visit he is turned away; Lucetta sends word that she is engaged. This irritates Henchard, who determines not to return the following day, as requested.

Elizabeth-Jane and Lucetta have become friends; the latter reveals part of her history and comes to believe that Henchard's cool feelings towards his daughter explain the mayor's reluctance to visit her. On market day she sends Elizabeth on an errand to get her out of the house, also sending a note to Henchard, hoping that he will visit while she is alone. However, when a gentleman caller is announced, it is not Henchard.

> Business and personal concerns are linked again. Lucetta's window, which overlooks the market place, has become a focal point. Two more important letters are written, revealing Lucetta's dangerous impulsiveness. We are likely to feel critical of her manipulation of Elizabeth-Jane, especially when she considers how best to 'get rid of' the girl (p. 152) so that Henchard can be induced to call. Lucetta's artful dressing, dramatic posturing and hysterical sobbing all suggest that she should be viewed as inferior to her companion, in spite of the attractions she possesses. But there is a measure of sympathy for her. She endured a 'flighty and unsettled' (p. 148) upbringing and clearly craves security. Henchard's feelings about Lucetta are mixed. Hardy emphasises the 'emotional void' (p. 145) in him, but indicates that he is prepared to marry primarily out of a sense of duty, not because he is deeply in love. We might feel that this union represents an acceptable business proposition for Henchard. His stubborn refusal to call on Lucetta until he is ready will have serious consequences. The chapter ends on a dramatic and intriguing note, with the unnamed male caller.

étourderie lack of thought
Titian well-known Venetian painter
the weak Apostle Peter (Matthew 26:73)

> **carrefour** (French) crossroads
> **Candlemas fair** the most important hiring fair in the agricultural year, held on 2 February
> **cyma-recta** an architectural term; describes the curve on cornice moulding

CHAPTER 23   **Farfrae and Lucetta are mutually attracted. Henchard is rebuffed**

The caller is revealed as Farfrae, who has come to visit Elizabeth-Jane. Lucetta engages him in conversation and the pair are attracted to one another. The Candlemas fair is in progress outside. Observing from the window, Farfrae overhears a conversation and goes out to offer employment to a young man who would otherwise have been forced to leave his sweetheart and father in order to work elsewhere. This generosity impresses Lucetta. Having completely forgotten about Elizabeth-Jane, Farfrae takes his leave. He has agreed to call on Lucetta again. Shortly after his departure Henchard arrives, but Lucetta again declines to see him, pleading a headache. She decides that Elizabeth-Jane might be useful as 'a watch-dog to keep her father off' (p. 162).

Farfrae's visit is **ironic**: he comes in search of the 'pleasing, thrifty and satisfactory' (p. 156) Elizabeth-Jane and leaves infatuated with the deceptive Lucetta. The fact that he forgets Elizabeth-Jane suggests that the unfortunate girl's destiny is to be disregarded. Lucetta's and Farfrae's characters are revealed through their dialogue and in spite of Lucetta's claim that she is not a coquette, she spends a good deal of time talking about love. She takes the lead and has a dramatic effect on Donald; he begins to wish that 'there were no business in the warrld' (p. 160)·and sentimentally hires the young man. Both 'lovers' display impulsiveness. Henchard is reduced to the role of helpless bystander – like Elizabeth-Jane – when he is turned away again. His star continues to wane.

> **Hyperborean** northern
> **kerseymere** fine wool
> **waggon-tilts** canvas covering for wagons
> **Lady-day** 25 March, the feast of the Annunciation of the Virgin Mary

CHAPTER 24   Lucetta and Henchard finally meet. Elizabeth-Jane
learns more of her friend's past

Lucetta and Elizabeth-Jane spend their days watching from the windows, hoping for glimpses of Farfrae. One Saturday a new seeding machine (a horse-drill) is brought to the market, attracting much attention. Lucetta and Elizabeth-Jane go out to examine it. They bump into Henchard, who ridicules the horse-drill and leaves swiftly. Elizabeth-Jane overhears Henchard quietly reproaching Lucetta for not seeing him. Farfrae defends the drill stoutly (it is his innovation) and Elizabeth-Jane realises that the young Scot and Lucetta enjoy a mutual attraction.

A few days later Lucetta tells Elizabeth-Jane a story about a woman who promised to marry one man but then found herself attracted to another. In spite of her attempts to conceal the fact that the 'she' she discusses is herself, Lucetta does not fool her companion, who instantly recognises that Lucetta is talking about her own predicament.

> The narrator confirms that a 'malignant star' (p. 165) is controlling Elizabeth's fate. It is **ironic** that Henchard believes that Farfrae and Elizabeth-Jane's courtship must be progressing when the former's attraction to Lucetta is growing. The seed-drill **symbolises** the contrast between Henchard and Farfrae; old-fashioned ways are being replaced by progressive methods. Again, in spite of her dazzling finery, we are likely to feel critical of Lucetta. Hardy allows us to see her through Elizabeth-Jane's 'sage' (p. 173) eyes, which serves to make us admire the younger girl more. We are offered a description of the Casterbridge evening market; as usual, trade provides the backdrop for romance (see Textual Analysis – Text 1 for a detailed discussion of a passage from this chapter).

the Heptarchy Saxon England
'Lass of Gowrie' a popular Scottish song
'He that observeth ... shall not sow' see Ecclesiastes 11:4

CHAPTER 25   Henchard proposes to Lucetta, who is evasive

Farfrae and Henchard continue to call on Lucetta, ignoring Elizabeth-Jane, who accepts their indifference stoically. Henchard speaks to Lucetta alone and asks her to marry him, but she responds evasively. His attitude towards her is possessive and domineering. He begins to sense that he must have a rival for Lucetta's affections, but does not know yet that it is Donald. Henchard comes to see that his manners and deportment do not 'fit' in Lucetta's drawing room: he lacks the fashionable and genteel qualities that she has come to prize. After Henchard's proposal Lucetta is even more determined that she would prefer Farfrae as a husband.

> Henchard's belief that Lucetta is 'almost his property' (p. 175) recalls the auction; however, we are likely to sympathise with him in this chapter because of his open 'chagrin' (p. 176), 'perceptible loss of power' (p. 175) and discomfort in the drawing room. There is a cruel **irony** in the fact that Lucetta's 'slight inaccessibility' inflames Henchard's 'smouldering sentiments' (p. 174); the repeated references to fire in relation to the former mayor suggest both destruction and passion. With ironic timing, Farfrae passes beneath the window in 'a yellow flood of reflected sunlight' (p. 177) just as Henchard is trying to pin down the evasive Lucetta. Her desire for security is emphasised; she is willing to take a tradesman who is beneath her socially in an attempt to win some happiness. Elizabeth-Jane's predicament – she is now 'invisible' (p. 174) – continues to evoke sympathy; unlike the characters, the reader fully appreciates her worth (because of the narrator's comments).

> **Protean variety** in Greek myth Proteus, an old man of the sea, could change his shape at will
> **'meaner beauties of the night'** from Sir Henry Wotton's (1568–1639) 'On his Mistress, the Queen of Bohemia'

CHAPTER 26   **Henchard engages and then fires Jopp. His business plans go awry**

Henchard realises that Farfrae is his rival when he and Donald meet at Lucetta's home. Observing them at tea Elizabeth-Jane considers the foolishness of their – and Lucetta's – behaviour. Henchard is now bent on destroying Farfrae commercially, hiring Jopp to assist him with his vengeful plan. Jopp is a willing accomplice, since he considers that the Scot took 'his' job as manager earlier. Elizabeth-Jane tries to warn

Henchard that Jopp is not trustworthy but is rebuffed. Henchard visits a local weather prophet, Fall, who predicts bad weather at harvest time. Acting on this prediction Henchard buys up large quantities of grain, believing that there will be a shortage in the autumn. However, the late summer weather is good and prices fall. Henchard is forced to sell his grain at a low price in order to meet his bills, and also has to borrow money from the bank. Angry and bitter, Henchard dismisses Jopp, who vows to be revenged on his unfortunate employer.

> Rivalry in love temporarily replaces business rivalry and Henchard's judgement falters, signified by his hiring of Jopp. Even Lucetta's house seems to reject Henchard. Both he and Farfrae appear ridiculous through the narrator's descriptions of the tea table; the broken bread is a **symbol** of their rivalry. Lucetta's fragility is conveyed through the use of a **simile**; her glance flits to Farfrae's eyes 'like a bird to its nest' (p. 181). We see that she lacks Elizabeth-Jane's stoicism and strength. The disclosure of Jopp's Jersey connection hints at trouble to come. Hardy shows his knowledge of an interest in country folklore in his description of the visit to Fall; this episode also reaffirms Henchard's fetishistic nature. When the weather – which is always significant in this novel – goes against him again we might feel that the protagonist is now doomed to failure in all areas of his life.

Tuscan painting painting of the Florentine school
pis aller (French) last resource
Alastor a god of revenge
like Saul at his reception by Samuel see 1 Samuel 9
the evil scrofula, tuberculosis of the lymphatic glands
dung-mixen a dunghill
living in Revelations this reference suggests turmoil and upheaval
(Revelations 16:18)

CHAPTER 27   **Henchard extracts a promise of marriage from Lucetta**

In contrast to Henchard, Farfrae has good fortune at harvest time. When the weather worsens he is able to make a substantial profit on the grain he has bought. There is an accident involving Farfrae's and Henchard's hay wagons outside Lucetta's house; Henchard's man is blamed. On the same evening Henchard follows Lucetta when she goes out to meet Donald and overhears part of their conversation, in which the couple declare their love. When she returns home Henchard confronts Lucetta and threatens to disclose her past if she will not agree to marry him. Elizabeth-Jane, who is puzzled by the hold Henchard appears to have over Lucetta, is a witness to this encounter.

> Rivalry dominates this chapter, driving Henchard to cruel treatment of Lucetta. The wagoners' clash foreshadows the physical fight between Henchard and Farfrae in Chapter 38. The location of this altercation, a spot associated with bear baiting and the town stocks, is significant: suggestive of the former mayor's continued humiliation. The narrator's comment, that 'the momentum of his character knew no patience' (p. 190) suggests the inevitability of Henchard's decline; both character and fate appear to be working against him now. Although Lucetta's duplicity helps us sympathise with him, his attempt to blackmail a woman who, as Elizabeth-Jane says 'cannot bear much' (p. 196), goes against Henchard. Lucetta's faint prepares us for her seizure and death later in the novel. Her final piece of dialogue, which closes the chapter, is anxious and fatalistic.

> **the Capitol** a hill in Rome; the temple of Jupiter stood here; defeated leaders were forced to follow behind their victors in Roman triumphal processions
>
> **zwailing** wandering aimlessly
>
> **gawk-hammer** stupid
>
> **giddying worm** a parasite which can cause death if consumed by sheep
>
> **shocks** sheaves of corn
>
> **lucubrations** night-time studies

CHAPTER 28   The furmity woman discloses Henchard's past

Henchard is called to stand in as a magistrate. The furmity woman has been charged with being a public nuisance. After the policeman gives evidence against her she tells the court that Henchard sold his wife twenty years earlier and therefore has no right to judge her. Henchard confirms her story and agrees with her assessment. Lucetta hears what has happened in court and is distressed: she did not know about the sale of Susan. She decides to leave for Port Bredy for a few days. Henchard attempts to call on Lucetta a number of times and learns that she has taken a walk on the turnpike road, towards Port Bredy shortly after her return.

This short chapter is a turning point for Henchard. The initial satirical humour of the Petty Sessions makes the furmity woman's revelation more dramatic; Henchard's quiet corroboration of her story is equally arresting, but it is not out of character. For all his faults, the former mayor is essentially an honest man. Gossip plays an important role when Lucetta learns the truth about Henchard's union with Susan. The timing of this revelation is, of course, **ironic**; just as she has agreed to marry Henchard he is publicly disgraced. The fact that his past has caught up with him suggests that Lucetta's secrets will probably be disclosed too. Hardy leaves us in suspense, wondering about the purpose of Lucetta's visit to Port Bredy. We assume that Henchard's attempts to call on Lucetta are driven by a desire to explain his actions.

Shallow and Silence corrupt, inept justices in *Henry IV, Part 2*

ashlar square blocks of stone, roughly hewn

the country of the Psalmist ... 'thou crownest the year with thy goodness, and thy paths drop fatness' (Psalm 65:11)

wambling walking unsteadily

turmit-head turnip-head, simpleton

larry commotion

CHAPTER 29   Henchard rescues Lucetta and Elizabeth-Jane from an enraged bull

Walking along the turnpike road to meet Farfrae, Lucetta encounters Elizabeth-Jane. The two women are suddenly confronted by a bull, which chases them towards a barn. As they are attempting to evade their adversary Henchard appears – looking for Lucetta – and rescues them. He escorts Lucetta home while Elizabeth-Jane offers to find her friend's lost muff and make her own way back to Casterbridge. On the way she is given a lift by Farfrae, who is returning from Port Bredy. Arriving home, Henchard offers to postpone their marriage, but Lucetta reveals that she has just wed Farfrae. Henchard is furious that she has broken her promise and Lucetta pleads with him not to tell Donald about her past.

There are further examples of mistiming. Lucetta meets Elizabeth-Jane on the road just when she hopes to greet her new husband and Henchard's suggestion of a long engagement is made after Lucetta and Donald have married. The sensational episode with the bull confirms Elizabeth-Jane's strength of character and reinforces our sense of Lucetta's weakness; the latter is besieged in this chapter, forced to reveal her marriage in the most trying circumstances before running off in desperation. Henchard displays some of his best qualities early in the chapter: he is gentle, courageous, selfless and heroic until he is 'idiotised' (p. 209) by Lucetta's news. We are likely to feel there is some justification for his outburst, 'Oh, you false woman!' (p. 210); a chance of happiness again eludes him. Henchard is like the bull he subdues: he is wounded and trapped. It is **ironic** that Grower – Henchard's chief creditor – should be the witness to Farfrae and Lucetta's marriage.

Abrahamic success Abraham had many children (Genesis 17:4)

Yahoo creatures in Book 4 of Swift's *Gulliver's Travels* (1726), which have human shapes and animal vices

the Thames Tunnel a 1300 ft tunnel under the Thames, opened in 1843

Gurth's collar of brass Gurth was a Saxon swineherd in Scott's *Ivanhoe* (1819)

CHAPTER 30   Elizabeth-Jane moves to lodgings

When she learns about Lucetta's marriage Elizabeth-Jane decides that she must leave High Street Hall. Ironically, she attempts to convince Lucetta that the only honourable match she can make is with Henchard during the conversation that reveals the marriage. Farfrae makes preparations to move into High Street Hall.

We focus on Elizabeth-Jane, whose desire for respectability (described by the narrator as 'almost vicious', p. 213) prompts her to move into lodgings. Her dogmatism is similar to Henchard's and it seems appropriate that her new home is closer to his. Some critics are unconvinced by the narrator's insistence that Elizabeth-Jane is unaware of the furmity woman's courtroom revelation. The young woman's 'grand control' (p. 214) contrasts with Lucetta's self-absorbed outbursts of feeling. We are perhaps becoming less sympathetic towards Farfrae; he understands that Elizabeth-Jane is attracted to him but does not consider how she might feel about sharing a house with him and his bride.

John Gilpin a Cheapside linen draper in William Cowper's poem, 'The Diverting History of John Gilpin' (1782)

... like the Apostle Paul 'For the good that I would I do not; but the evil which I would not, that I do' (Romans 7:19)

in Nathan tones David arranged the death of Uriah the Hittite so that he could marry his widow, who was already pregnant by him. The prophet Nathan condemned him in an accusatory tone and David was then cursed by God (Samuel 12:1–14)

CHAPTER 31   **Bankrupt, Henchard moves to Jopp's cottage. Farfrae buys up his business**

Now that the sale of his wife has become common knowledge, Henchard's reputation is ruined and his creditors press in upon him. He is declared bankrupt, but behaves with great dignity. He moves into Jopp's cottage near Priory Mill. When she hears of his predicament Elizabeth-Jane attempts to visit and comfort him, but Henchard will not see her. Passing the location of his former business she discovers that Donald Farfrae has bought the premises and kept Henchard's employees on. The men are happier working for the Scot; although wages are lower, conditions are better.

Henchard again loses everything in an auction. The reversal of fortunes is rapid, but the former mayor retains his dignity because of his generous behaviour; as the Commissioner says, 'I can see every attempt has been made to avoid wronging anybody' (p. 217). We sympathise with Henchard because he punishes himself, going into self-imposed exile with a man he hates. His refusal to see Elizabeth-Jane suggests that Henchard is bent on isolating himself further. Finally, the narrator stresses that the townsfolk regret his downfall, even though the men who used to work for him are generally happier under Farfrae. We perhaps feel critical of the Scot for paying a lower wage. In subsequent chapters Hardy will continue to make Farfrae less attractive as he builds sympathy for his flawed hero.

Boldwood a character who appears as a suitor to the heroine Bathsheba Everdene in *Far from the Madding Crowd* (1874)

arch-labels mouldings over doors and windows

cat-head a beam that hangs over a well; a pulley is attached to it

CHAPTER 32   **Farfrae and Lucetta buy Henchard's old house. Henchard is offered employment by Farfrae**

Depressed, Henchard haunts one of the bridges on the outskirts of Casterbridge. He thinks of emigrating. One day he meets Jopp at the most distant bridge; his former employee takes sadistic pleasure in telling him that Farfrae has purchased his former home and furniture. Henchard then encounters Farfrae in the same location; Farfrae offers him a room in his old house and tells him that he is welcome to take back his furniture, but Henchard refuses these offers. He realises that he might have wronged Farfrae. When Henchard falls ill he is cared for by Elizabeth-Jane. On his recovery he decides to apply to Farfrae for work as a hay-trusser. To begin with he is able to accept his new role as employee, but Farfrae's continued success rankles. At the end of the chapter Elizabeth-Jane learns that Henchard has 'busted out drinking' again when his vow of temperance comes to an end.

This chapter concludes the reversal of fortunes. The sombre setting of the bridges reflects Henchard's mood; when the former mayor learns that Farfrae has bought up his furniture and moved into his house Hardy describes how 'the low land grew blacker, and the sky a deeper grey' (p. 223). Henchard and Farfrae reverse roles too; the former considers emigrating, while the latter extends the hand of friendship, although we might feel that he is insensitive when he offers Henchard his own furniture with these words: 'I will have plenty of opportunities of getting more' (p. 225). The news that

Farfrae might be made mayor is a mighty blow to Henchard's self-esteem, which leads to his degeneration through drink. His return to drinking might also be seen as defiant; although Henchard is to a certain extent 'broken in' (p. 226), he remains vengeful and still sports the clothes he wore during his heyday. We come to see Elizabeth-Jane as a possible source of hope and redemption; here she is associated with 'rapid recovery' (p. 225).

Adonis a handsome youth beloved by the goddess Venus

journey-work work paid by the day

the Prophet's chamber the prophet referred to is Elisha (Kings 4:10)

she was wise in her generation this is a reference to the parable of the unjust steward, who cheats his master (Luke 16:8)

CHAPTER 33   **Henchard's bitterness grows**

Henchard begins drinking again at The King of Prussia. In a belligerent mood he forces the town choir to sing Psalm 109, which includes a curse against men who enjoy ill-gotten riches. When Lucetta and Farfrae pass by it becomes clear that the psalm is intended as a threat against them. At this point Elizabeth-Jane arrives and diffuses the situation by escorting Henchard home. She offers to help him with his hay-trussing, since Henchard is finding Abel Whittle's pitying looks increasingly unendurable. Lucetta inadvertently comes across Henchard at work in the yard: he is sarcastic to her. She sends him a letter of reproach, which he destroys, although Henchard knows that he could have used it to compromise Lucetta. In her role as peacemaker Elizabeth-Jane has taken to bringing Henchard tea (to keep him away from alcohol). One day she arrives and finds Henchard and Farfrae standing close to the edge of the outer doorway on the upper floor of the corn-stores; she is perturbed when she notices Henchard raising his hand, as if he wishes to push Farfrae out. Elizabeth-Jane decides that she must caution Farfrae about Henchard.

Hardy shows his interest in history, customs and local Casterbridge life at the beginning of the chapter; he also carefully delineates the social hierarchy in the town. The psalm shows Henchard's extreme bitterness and its last verse **foreshadows** his dying wishes.

Henchard now suggests that Farfrae bewitched him with his singing, as if he were a siren pulling him to his doom: it is clear that Henchard blames the Scot for his misfortunes. The former mayor displays his worst qualities here: he is an aggressive, sarcastic bully and we have some sympathy with the hapless Lucetta, who is still addicted to dangerous letter writing. To his credit Henchard burns this missive. We see Lucetta and Donald through Elizabeth-Jane's wise onlooker's eyes: the new bride clings to her husband; she knows her happiness is precarious. The chapter closes on a silent, uneasy note, with Elizabeth-Jane 'quite sick at heart' (p. 236). Henchard's physical strength is emphasised throughout this chapter and his raised arm is an ominous sign that further trouble will soon occur.

Stonehenge the most famous Bronze Age temple in Europe, it lies on Salisbury Plain. Hardy uses Stonehenge as a setting when his heroine is arrested in *Tess of the d'Urbervilles*

rantipole wild

Rogue's March the tune played when a soldier received a dishonourable discharge

fourth Psa'am 'the Lord will hear when I call him' ... 'I will lay me down in peace, and sleep; for thou, Lord, only makest me dwell in safety'

old Wiltshire a hymn tune composed by Sir George Smart (1776–1867)

Rosalind's exclamation ... see *As You Like It*, III.5, in which Rosalind ticks off the shepherdess Phoebe for scorning the love of the shepherd Silvius

CHAPTER 34   Elizabeth-Jane warns Farfrae of Henchard's anger.
Lucetta asks Henchard to return her letters

Elizabeth-Jane discloses her fears about Henchard, but Farfrae does not take her seriously. However, when the town clerk informs him that Henchard hates him Farfrae decides not to go ahead with a personal scheme to set his rival up in a seed shop. Henchard is informed – wrongly – that Farfrae vetoed the council's plan to install him in the shop. Lucetta tries to persuade Donald to sell up and leave Casterbridge, but when the mayor dies suddenly her husband accepts the nomination to succeed him. Lucetta then asks Henchard to return her letters, which are still in the safe of his former home. Calling to collect them one evening, Henchard tantalisingly reads sections of them to Farfrae, without revealing the name of the writer.

The reading of Lucetta's love letters provides some moments of grim humour and irony and proves that Henchard is not capable of carrying through acts of premeditated malice; he is decent in spite of himself. This is shown again in Chapter 38 when he is unable to push Farfrae out of the loft. Farfrae, though generous, does not understand his former employer, shown by the way he speaks to him with the 'cheeriness of a superior' (p. 237). It is ironic that he shows little interest in hearing the letters read, and then feels that the tone of the writing reminds him of his wife. Poor Lucetta's hopes are dashed: just as she tries to persuade Donald to leave Casterbridge Dr Chalkfield dies and Farfrae is offered the position of mayor, a post which would, ironically, appeal to the socially ambitious wife in other circumstances. With his elevation to mayor, it seems that Farfrae's triumph is complete.

worm i' the bud see *Twelfth Night*, II.4, in which Viola (disguised as Cesario) describes the way in which her 'sister' pined away because she could not declare her love (Viola is describing her own love for Orsino): 'She never told her love,/ But let concealment, like a worm i' the bud,/ Feed on her damask cheek'
Tamarlane's trumpet the soldiers of Tamburlaine, the great Mongolian conqueror, were said to carry large trumpets
Aphrodite the Greek goddess of love

CHAPTER 35   Henchard meets Lucetta at the Ring

Lucetta overheard Henchard reading from her letters. The morning afterwards she writes anxiously to Henchard requesting a meeting at the Ring. At the rendezvous that evening she deliberately makes herself look plain and careworn; her appearance and subdued demeanour remind Henchard of his previous meeting with Susan and make him feel sympathetic towards Lucetta. He agrees to return the letters the next day.

The language used to describe Lucetta's feelings and actions continues to convey desperation. She fears the revelation of her past will prove 'fatal' (p. 245), and wonders how she can 'parry'

CHAPTER 35 continued

Henchard's 'incipient attack' (p. 246). We feel a good deal of sympathy for her as she goes to the Ring, which is lit by a sun which aptly resembles 'a drop of blood on an eyelid' (p. 247). When Henchard sees her he decides that Lucetta is 'very small deer to hunt' (p. 248). This **metaphor** conveys Lucetta's vulnerability. Ironically, it is the memory of a similar furtive meeting in the past that persuades Henchard to keep Lucetta's secrets. Lucetta's careworn appearance evokes sympathy; she is losing the looks she set so much store by. Henchard's gentleness helps to redeem his character after the brutal actions of the previous chapter, and we will trust him when he says he can keep his word.

CHAPTER 36   Henchard asks Jopp to deliver the letters to Lucetta

Returning home Lucetta meets Jopp, who asks her to recommend him to her husband. She refuses rather brusquely, saying that she does not meddle in Farfrae's business affairs. Later Henchard asks Jopp to deliver the bundle of letters to Lucetta. Jopp agrees. On his errand he meets some friends and they repair to an inn in Mixen Lane for a drink. Here the letters are opened and read publicly. Nance Mockridge suggests a skimmity-ride. A stranger hears this discussion and offers a sovereign to help cover the costs of this 'entertainment'. When she receives the letters from Jopp Lucetta burns them; **ironically** believing that her past will now remain a secret.

Mixen Lane and the customers of Saint Peter's Finger are described in detail; it is appropriate that this seedy location, associated with furtive behaviour, villainy and degradation is the setting in which Lucetta's unmasking is planned. It is also appropriate that the furmity woman should make her final appearance here. Henchard's failure to seal the bundle of letters recalls Susan's earlier failure, and again the results are disastrous. There are two important chance meetings: Jopp comes across Mother Cuxsom and Nance Mockridge and Newson reappears at the inn. Hardy does not reveal his identity at this point, in order to add suspense to an already ominous chapter. Knowing how vulnerable Lucetta is we are unlikely to share the townsfolk's perception of the skimmington-ride as offering an opportunity for 'a good laugh'

(p. 258) (see Textual Analysis – Text 2 for a detailed discussion of the introduction to Mixen Lane).

Adullam Saul takes refuge in Adullam in Canaan when he flees David's wrath (1 Samuel 22:2)
like Ashton at the disappearance of Ravenswood a reference to Scott's *The Bride of Lammermoor* (1819). In Chapter 34 Colonel Ashton watches as Ravenswood sinks into quicksand

CHAPTER 37   Henchard causes a scene during a royal visit: the skimmity-ride is planned

A royal personage is due to pass through Casterbridge. Henchard hopes that he can be a member of the welcoming party but is not allowed to participate because he is no longer a councillor. However, when the visit occurs he intrudes, stepping forward in his shabby clothes and waving a home-made Union Jack. Farfrae – now mayor – immediately pushes Henchard back into the crowd. We learn that the skimmity-ride will take place that night. Two men (Longways and Coney) decide to warn the parties concerned in advance by sending letters.

Henchard is a rather pathetic and ridiculous figure in this chapter, shabby and fuelled by drink. His brief public tussle with Farfrae will lead to a more serious private confrontation later on, just as the superficial pomp of the royal visit will give way to the deadly skimmington ride. It is ironic that Lucetta means to know Henchard in public no more, and will shortly be coupled with him in effigy. In spite of the sympathy and concern shown by Coney and Longways, we know that the lower orders will have the final word. Farfrae and Lucetta are already past the zenith of their popularity; shortly their social standing will be undermined in a very cruel way.

the third king George George III (1760–1820)
fête carillonée a festival marked by the peal of bells
Calphurnia's cheek was pale see *Julius Caesar*. Calpurnia pales when Caesar has an epileptic fit when he is warned to 'Beware the Ides of March'
Pharaoh's chariots reference to the Egyptian army pursuing the Israelites as they cross the Red Sea (Exodus 14:25)
mandy insolent, saucy

hontish proud

toppered brought down

CHAPTER 38   **Farfrae and Henchard fight at the corn-stores**

Bent on revenge, Henchard asks Farfrae to meet him at the corn-stores, intending to wrestle and kill him. He ties one arm behind his back so that the fight may be considered fair. Henchard has his enemy at his mercy, but finds himself unable to push Farfrae out of the loft doorway to his death. Having let him go he lies down in the corner, reproaching himself for his violent outburst. When he recovers, Farfrae continues towards Weatherbury to keep an unexpected appointment (he had been on his way to Budmouth). Henchard is struck by a desire to see him again and beg his pardon. While waiting for Farfrae's return he wanders the streets, eventually arriving at the stone bridge he has lingered at before. He hears a noise coming from the town but does not know what it signifies.

> Henchard, who feels he has been made to look like a 'vagabond' (p. 266), reaches the depths of degradation when he almost becomes a murderer. Hardy contrasts Farfrae – the 'fair and slim antagonist' (p. 269) – with the more powerful Henchard, who is 'Prince of Darkness' (p. 269). But superior strength debases Henchard; after the 'mad attack' (p. 271) in the loft he is described as tragically womanly. This description points to his later subjugation to Elizabeth-Jane. As usual, Henchard immediately regrets his rashness, but we know that reparation is impossible. Hardy maintains suspense: Henchard is the only character who knows Farfrae's destination.

> **Weltlust** an enjoyment in worldly pleasure
>
> **'And here's a hand ...'** from Robert Burns's 'Auld Lang Syne'

CHAPTER 39   **Lucetta witnesses the skimmity-ride and falls into a fit**

We learn that Farfrae has been diverted to Weatherbury after receiving a note. This is to ensure that he is out of the way during the skimmity-ride. While she waits for her husband's return Lucetta hears the noise of the ride and two maidservants in conversation; they are discussing the figures in the procession. Elizabeth-Jane arrives and tries to dissuade Lucetta from watching the skimmity-ride, but it is too late. When she sees the effigies Lucetta becomes hysterical and falls down in an epileptic fit. A doctor is summoned. He fears that Lucetta's condition is serious and tells Farfrae's man to fetch him from Budmouth (where he is assumed to have gone). Meanwhile the Casterbridge constables are unable to apprehend the perpetrators of the skimmity-ride, who have made themselves scarce.

> There is tragic **irony** in the fact that Lucetta feels most happy and secure on the night of her death. (Indeed, it might be implied in the phrase 'the present state of her health' that she is pregnant.) Some critics see her demise as the climax of the Farfrae–Henchard struggle. Hardy carefully builds up to the skimmington ride through the dialogue of two observers watching from windows and offers both visual and aural details, as well as descriptions of Lucetta's frantic reactions. As usual Elizabeth-Jane plays the role of guardian, but her entrance occurs too late. Ironically, as Lucetta falls to the ground the noise of the skimmington-ride ceases. The constables, who are compared with the ineffectual Dogberry and Verges from *Much Ado About Nothing*, are no match for the duplicity of the denizens of Mixen Lane. It is sadly appropriate that their cunning unmasks Lucetta, whose attempts at secrecy have proved unsuccessful. In spite of the humour introduced by the constables we are unlikely to feel much relief at the end of this chapter.

crouds fiddles
serpents wind instruments
felo de se (Latin) suicide
like the crew of *Comus* in Milton's masque *Comus* (1634) Comus is a pagan god of mirth, his 'crew' are a group of rowdy monsters

CHAPTER 40   **Henchard tries to tell Farfrae that Lucetta is dangerously ill, but he refuses to believe him. Lucetta dies**

Henchard has also witnessed the skimmity-ride and immediately makes his way to Lucetta's house. When he learns of her illness he tries to inform people of Farfrae's destination, but is not believed. So he sets out to find Farfrae himself. He encounters him on the road, but the Scotsman refuses to believe what he hears and continues on his errand. Henchard is wretched. He calls at her house to enquire about Lucetta's progress during the night. When he finally returns home Donald sits up with Lucetta, who confesses her past relationship with Henchard. When Henchard reaches his lodgings Jopp informs him that a sea-captain has been enquiring after him. Unable to rest he paces up and down outside Farfrae's house. At dawn he learns that Lucetta has died.

Henchard's guilty sadness is reiterated many times in this chapter; he moves from 'grave reflection' (p. 280) to 'a state of bitter anxiety and contrition' (p. 281), until he is 'almost bowed down with despair' (p. 282). **Ironically**, he behaves most nobly and generously when he has 'lost his good name' (p. 281); when he is most honest Henchard is disbelieved. His agony becomes heroic; his heart-rending and humble plea to 'Mr. Farfrae', 'I am a wretched man, but my heart is true to you still' (p. 282) is akin to some of Lear's plaintive outbursts in *King Lear*. But it is too late. We might feel critical of Farfrae for being so preoccupied with business, but we can understand his lack of trust. At the end of the chapter Henchard's thoughts turn to Elizabeth-Jane; Hardy is preparing us for her pre-eminence in the final chapters of the novel. She is now seen by the desolate Henchard as 'a pin-point of light' (p. 283) in his dark existence.

no joy in heaven '... joy shall be in heaven over one sinner that repenteth, more than over ninety and nine persons, which need no repentance' (Luke 15:7)

a less scrupulous Job Job, volatile, but characteristically patient and righteous, endures a number of afflictions (much worse than Henchard's) and curses himself (Job 3:1–10)

Lucifer the planet Venus when it appears as the morning star

CHAPTER 41   Newson comes to Casterbridge looking for Susan and
              Elizabeth-Jane. Henchard tells him both women are
              dead

The morning that Lucetta dies Elizabeth-Jane visits Henchard. While
she sleeps, he prepares breakfast for her. Newson calls and Henchard tells
him that Susan and his daughter are dead: he fears losing the 'daughter'
he has come to love. Upset, Newson leaves Casterbridge. However,
Henchard fears that the sailor will return and regrets his lies. He makes
his way to the weir, intending to drown himself. When he sees the effigy
of himself floating in the water he takes this as an sign that he should not
attempt to destroy himself. Henchard returns to Elizabeth-Jane and the
two are reconciled; the girl offers to live with her 'father' again.

> Ironically, just as there is a reconciliation between Henchard and
> Elizabeth-Jane, Newson reappears. Some critics find his credulity
> improbable, while others suggest that it is in keeping with the
> youthful naïveté he displays in Chapter 1. Henchard's desperation
> dominates this chapter. It is demonstrated most dramatically when
> he tells 'mad lies' 'like a child' (p. 289); it is intolerable that the
> 'honour' (p. 286) of caring for Elizabeth-Jane should be snatched
> away. We both sympathise with and condemn Henchard's actions,
> which are motivated by deep loneliness and love. The former mayor
> is a diminished figure; he waits on his stepdaughter and is afraid of
> displeasing her; this idea is developed further in the next chapter. It
> seems very sad that an effigy prevents Henchard from committing
> suicide and bitterly ironic that Elizabeth-Jane should now wish to
> live with him.

CHAPTER 42   Henchard and Elizabeth-Jane live comfortably
              together, but he feels threatened when he discovers
              that Farfrae and Elizabeth-Jane are courting

Elizabeth-Jane and Henchard are set up in the seed shop by the Town
Council. As time passes they prosper. However, Henchard is
disconcerted when he learns that Elizabeth-Jane and Farfrae are growing
increasingly attached to one another again. He spies on the couple and
thinks about telling Donald that Elizabeth-Jane is illegitimate, but does
not meddle, in spite of his fear of losing his 'daughter'.

This is a quiet chapter which prepares us for the novel's final dramatic events. Ironically, given her sensational and unexpected death, life in Casterbridge goes on as if Lucetta had never lived. Henchard's peace of mind has been destroyed and he again fears the revelation of his past actions; we are told that 'the apparition of Newson haunted him' (p. 295). In spite of this he enjoys working and living with Elizabeth-Jane, until he is again seized by the 'burning, jealous dread of rivalry' (p. 296) when he realises that Farfrae is interested in his stepdaughter. More than anything, Henchard – a 'netted lion' (p. 297) - fears losing the girl who has 'her own way in everything now' (p. 296). Although we will feel glad that Henchard has finally found and experienced a more selfless love, it is impossible not to feel that he is a diminished figure. The narrator says that he is 'denaturalized' (p. 299), a word which suggests loss. Farfrae is also chastened; he reflects coolly on his marriage to Lucetta, as befits a businessman (does his pragmatism make him a less attractive character?). He also sums up one of the themes of the novel when he says, 'Ah, I doubt there will be any good in secrets! A secret cast a deep shadow over my life' (p. 300). These words could be applied to all the characters.

Juno's bird the goddess Juno had a sacred peacock

Argus eyes the giant Argos had 100 eyes, which were always open. When he was killed his eyes were put in the tail of Juno's peacock

solicitus timor (Latin) worrisome fear

locus standi (Latin) recognised position

CHAPTER 43   **Fearing the disclosure of his lies, Henchard leaves Casterbridge**

Elizabeth-Jane and Donald become the subject of gossip in Casterbridge; Henchard wonders what he should do when they marry. His main concern is to be able to remain near the girl. One day when he is out spying on the lovers he sees Newson heading towards the town. Henchard decides to leave Casterbridge. He departs as he arrived many years previously, dressed as a hay-trusser. Elizabeth-Jane sees him off with a heavy heart. Farfrae asks her to go to his house, where she is reunited with her real father, Newson. When she learns about Henchard's lies she feels bitter. Wedding preparations are underway.

The chapter opens with gossip; Elizabeth-Jane's superiority is finally – publicly – recognised, demonstrated by the discussion about her marrying Farfrae; in the words of the urban chorus, ''Tis she that's stooping to he' (p. 302). Thereafter the focus is on Henchard's acute suffering. He becomes 'morbidly sensitive' (p. 303) and misanthropic as Elizabeth draws closer to Farfrae, wishing to return to the obscurity of his early life. Still he is pummelled by opposing impulses; should he humiliate himself by staying on in Casterbridge or leave when his stepdaughter marries? He stoops to eavesdropping again and discovers that Newson has returned. This prompts Henchard to leave, keeping his final destructive secret. By this point we will probably feel that regardless of the mistakes he has made, Henchard is truly a tragic hero; he is stoical in his 'state of hopelessness' (p. 307). The narrator emphasises that the wheel has turned full circle; at the moment that he leaves the scene of his former glories, 'Henchard formed … much the same picture as he had presented when entering Casterbridge for the first time nearly a quarter of a century before' (pp. 306–7). Newson contrasts sharply with Henchard, and in spite of his display of physical affection, we might feel that his love for Elizabeth does not compare with Henchard's; Newson describes Henchard's lies rather curiously as a 'good joke' (p. 311). Any reservations we have about him here are reinforced when he moves to Budmouth only three days after the wedding in the final chapter; her stepfather can hardly bear to tear himself away from Elizabeth-Jane.

'the shade from his own soul upthrown' from Shelley's 'The Last Revolt of Islam' (1818)

Cain after he had killed his brother Abel, Cain was condemned by God to be 'a fugitive and a vagabond'. Cain said that this punishment was more than he could bear (Genesis 4:8–15)

CHAPTER 44   Elizabeth-Jane marries Donald

Henchard retraces his steps to Weydon-Priors, where he ponders the fateful wife-sale. He is also absorbed by thoughts of Elizabeth-Jane. He finds employment as a hay-trusser. Meanwhile Elizabeth-Jane marries Farfrae. Newson participates in the wedding celebrations.

> There is a sense of impending doom and deep sadness in the account of Henchard retracing his steps and reliving his past. He wants to die. Henchard continues to punish himself for the 'crime' (p. 313) he committed and remains contradictory to the end; sneering at himself for being drawn to Casterbridge, but unable to stop thinking about Elizabeth-Jane. The mementoes he carries (a curl of the girl's hair, her gloves etc.) are poignant symbols of love and loss. Henchard recognises the futility of his existence, while the narrator stresses the influence of 'the ingenious machinery contrived by the gods for reducing human possibilities of amelioration to a minimum' (p. 314). The contrast between Henchard's solitary wanderings and the wedding celebrations could not be more stark. Appropriately, Elizabeth-Jane wears a snowy white dress; descriptions of her and Farfrae suggest the harmony of their relationship. Unsurprisingly, Elizabeth is not energetic and effusive; even on her wedding day she displays only 'nervous pleasure' (p. 316). (In this version of his novel Hardy has deleted a section in which Henchard returns for the wedding, is greeted coldly by Elizabeth-Jane and departs, leaving a present of a finch in a cage, which is only later discovered when dead – see Appendix 1 of the Penguin Classics Edition.) The chapter closes with a brief description of the happy Newson, who provides another stark contrast to Henchard; the once great man is reduced to sleeping under hedges. We are being prepared for his death in rural desolation.

ballet-sheet ballad sheet
pari passu at the same speed

CHAPTER 45   Henchard dies in a derelict cottage

Shortly after the wedding Newson moves to Budmouth. Elizabeth-Jane settles into married life, but begins to wonder what has happened to

Henchard. She begs her husband to find out where he is so that she can do something to make his life more tolerable. Farfrae learns that he has been seen on the Melchester highway. After a journey which takes them across Egdon Heath, Elizabeth-Jane and Donald catch sight of Abel Whittle near a cottage in a ravine. When they enter the dwelling they learn that Henchard has just died there. Whittle describes Henchard's final days. His will, which has been written on a scrap of paper, hangs on the bedhead. Henchard's dying wish was that no-one should remember him. Elizabeth-Jane regrets not seeking her stepfather out sooner. Respecting his integrity she carries out the terms of Henchard's will.

Henchard can be compared to King Lear again in this chapter; his death in a ramshackle cottage attended by Whittle recalls Lear and his fool on the heath in Act III. It is appropriate that the humble Whittle should recount the story of the former mayor's final days; Henchard's life has gone full circle and he dies close to the location of his original sin, a lowly countryman once more. Whittle is a character of unaffected, natural sympathy, which makes his tale more moving. Elizabeth-Jane's silence conveys sorrow, regret and respect; it seems appropriate that she obeys the commands in Henchard's negative will. In this bitter document the former mayor reveals his wish to be obliterated, a desire which fits in with his urge to punish himself in life. The novel closes with an explanation of Elizabeth-Jane's moral philosophy and clear-headed outlook on life. Unlike all the other characters in the novel the young woman seems to have achieved a balanced view and recognises social ambition (which has been so destructive) as an unnecessary distraction; 'she could perceive no great personal difference between being respected in the nether parts of Casterbridge, and glorified at the uppermost end of the social world' (p. 322). Hardy's own philosophy of life seems to come across in the concluding paragraphs, when the narrator describes life as 'a brief transit through a sorry world' (p. 322) and happiness as 'the occasional episode in a general drama of pain' (p. 322). These pronouncements provide an appropriately pessimistic sense of **closure** (see Textual Analysis – Text 3 for a detailed discussion of the ending of the novel).

Crusoe in Defoe's *Robinson Crusoe* (1719) Crusoe was eventually rescued from years on a desert island after being shipwrecked

antipodean absences Australian prisons

to extenuate nothing see *Othello*, V.2 and Othello's final words before stabbing himself

Minerva-eyes a quotation from Shelley's 'The Revolt of Islam' (1818). Hardy suggests that Elizabeth has gained wisdom

Diana Multimammia Diana the many-breasted goddess of fertility

Capharnaum Capernaum, on the Sea of Galilee. Jesus started preaching here (Matthew 4:13–23 and 8:5–27). See also Isaiah 9:2, in which Capernaum is described as 'the land of the shadow of death'

PART THREE

CRITICAL APPROACHES

CHARACTERISATION

MICHAEL HENCHARD

Many critics feel that Hardy's portrayal of Michael Henchard is one of the most complex, fascinating and psychologically convincing character studies in Victorian literature. He has been compared to King Lear, Heathcliff and Trollope's Louis Trevelyan, the monomaniacal male protagonist in *He Knew He Was Right* (1869). A number of commentators have also suggested Henchard is a representative of the old rural ways that were dying out in the second half of the nineteenth century; in these readings of the novel he is Agricultural Man defeated. Hardy compares his protagonist to biblical and literary figures, Saul, Job and Faust. These titanic figures suggest the power of the man and his suffering.

Henchard is a character of contradictions and extremes. Even in the prologue he arouses mixed feelings. Throughout Chapter 1 he displays a range of negative traits: drunk and quarrelsome, he is a bully, and an irresponsible and cruel husband and father. Henchard is also impetuous, egotistical, volatile, bad tempered and overbearing. He does not appear to consider the consequences of his actions until it is too late. All these qualities remain part of his characterisation and are developed as events unfold. In Chapter 2 we see him as a man of determination, strength of character and pride. His dogged attempts to find Susan suggest that he desires to make reparation for his evil actions and possesses a sense of responsibility; the fact that he spends Newson's money on the search hints that he might also be capable of acts of selfless generosity. Again, these better qualities are developed in the rest of the novel, although many critics feel that Henchard is portrayed as a thoroughly bad man.

When we next see Henchard he has prospered. The title of the novel suggests that his social standing is of paramount importance to the tragic hero, and in worldly terms the mayor has triumphed. However, we quickly become aware that Henchard is extremely lonely, and the narrator suggests that he still possesses the same characteristics that were so alarming in the first chapter. Henchard's loneliness is revealed in all his relationships: he hires Farfrae partly because he reminds him of his dead brother; he forms and then pursues his liaison with Lucetta because he feels an emotional void; finally he clings to Elizabeth-Jane – the only creature who responds to him favourably. Henchard has worked so hard to rehabilitate himself through achieving business success (does he need to recover his self-esteem following the wife sale?) that he has had no time for close personal relationships. But even here there are contradictions: Henchard is a self-confessed woman hater, who needs to dominate others and demonstrate his power, and yet he craves company. As many critics have noted, it is as if the man is at war with himself.

This war is caused by contradictory impulses, and by the fact that Henchard's instincts are predominantly destructive. As noted above, Henchard the mayor is not so very different from Henchard the inebriated hay-trusser. Consider the narrator's description of the mayor presiding over the feast in Chapter 5: 'He had a rich complexion, which verged on swarthiness, a flashing black eye, and dark, bushy brows and hair.' Henchard only occasionally indulges in a loud laugh, and this laugh 'was not encouraging to strangers'. The narrator goes on to inform us that his laugh 'fell in well with conjectures of a temperament which would have no pity for weakness … Its producer's personal goodness, if he had any, would be of a very fitful cast – an occasional almost oppressive generosity rather than a mild and constant kindness' (Chapter 5, p. 32). It is clear that Henchard has achieved success through discipline; and as the events of the novel prove, it is a supreme effort of will for Henchard to control his destructive instincts. Other negative character traits that can be added to the list above include his propensity to love and hate without moderation, possessiveness, a competitive streak and a tendency towards self-pity. These qualities are displayed in his relationships with the other principal characters.

We are encouraged to believe that Henchard is destroyed by two elements: his character and fate. We might feel that time and the past play important roles in his demise. The narrator suggests that there is an inevitability about Henchard's fall: at times the elements go disastrously against him and he feels himself that there are malign forces at work in the universe (it could be argued that this is a sign of self-pity). Time and the past are linked; the pattern of the novel suggests that coincidental meetings and bad timing play a role in determining the characters' destinies, and Henchard is haunted by his past: it drives him to secrecy and deception, and as chance – or fate – would have it, he is not allowed to conceal his sins for ever. It is also possible to argue that Henchard is brought down by women. The reappearance of three women, Susan, Lucetta and the furmity woman, leads to dramatic revelations that disturb and then destroy him. We might even feel that his possessive love for Elizabeth-Jane contributes to his downfall; Henchard's lies to Newson lead to self-imposed exile and a lonely death. Some critics feel that Henchard dies of a broken heart.

His relationships with women reveal the contradictions in Henchard, as does his rivalry with Farfrae; for whom some suggest he feels a Freudian, unruly, homosexual love. Henchard is cruel and kind to those he loves; he is generous, tries to treat them fairly, but, when they disappoint him in some way, usually by not bending to his will, he lashes out. He is enraged by Susan's naïve assumption that the wife sale is binding, angry when he learns that Elizabeth-Jane is not his daughter, furious when Lucetta chooses another man and deeply hurt when Farfrae will no longer endure his temper. The narrator constantly stresses the mercantile way Henchard tries to relate to these other characters: he tries to 'buy' all the women at some stage and his personal antipathy to Farfrae leads to a commercial war. His interaction with Farfrae reveals his most destructive and violent tendencies; this relationship, which is the focus of the book, is doomed from the start. Although they share the tendency to act impulsively, these two men are fundamentally very different. Henchard's powerful love for the man who resembles his dead brother becomes passionate hatred. We will condemn many of Henchard's responses to Farfrae: his overbearing friendliness, the abrupt dismissal, his concerted attempts to undermine his business and personal affairs and his physical attack on the younger man. However, Farfrae never understands Henchard, as we can tell from the brief response he makes when his employer describes his periodic fits of gloom: 'Ah, now, I never feel like that' (Chapter 12, p. 77). This, along with his patronising treatment of Henchard later in the novel, will help us to view Henchard more favourably.

What other methods does Hardy employ to make us feel for his rigid and egotistical monster? Even if we do not approve of Henchard, we are encouraged to understand him because the narrator constantly offers us an insight into his feelings and motives. It is also true that his negative traits are compelling in a way the more virtuous Farfrae's character is not. And his positive characteristics, which become more obvious towards the end, evoke sympathy. Henchard begins to punish himself and exerts an enormous effort of will to control his impulses. It becomes apparent that he possesses good instincts in spite of himself, shown by his inability to reveal Lucetta's name when he reads aloud to Farfrae from her letters. Some suggest that Henchard becomes heroic and sympathetic in his degradation. His energy and determination, which previously led to destruction, enable him to endure and learn (although, we may argue about how much he learns; his lies to Newson suggest Henchard will never really adapt and change). As he becomes an onlooker, almost exchanging roles with Elizabeth-Jane, Henchard is forced to look inside himself. This is not entirely unexpected: his earlier regret after impulsive actions prepares us for his self-imposed exile. Before this he has acted in a selfless way that evokes pity on more than one occasion, for example, when he makes his frantic attempt to get Farfrae to return home in Chapter 40. The remorse and misery that Henchard shows in the final chapters make him a figure of **pathos**; his suffering is unendurable and yet he doggedly bears it. Critics have also suggested that Henchard becomes a more positive figure when he becomes more feminine: the description of him lying in the corner of the loft after the fight with Farfrae and his anxious attempts to please Elizabeth-Jane clearly depict this. Henchard becomes as anxious as Susan was early in the novel.

However, we might feel ambivalent about this change in Henchard. Is he diminished in the final chapters? The narrator tells us that Henchard has been 'denaturalized' (Chapter 42, p. 299); he becomes 'a fangless lion' (Chapter 43, p. 303). It is true that Henchard moves closer to Elizabeth-Jane through self-denial, but we might regret his subjugation. We must also consider his lonely death. Here Henchard seems to reassert his will; the document hanging over his deathbed could not be more vehement, although Henchard clearly wishes to obliterate all traces of himself. The fact that he is cared for by Whittle evokes sympathy, reminding us of Henchard's loss of power. Some critics suggest that Henchard's late focus on love and dying rejection of ambition make him sympathetic. Finally, the fact that Henchard has come full circle, ending up as he began, a homeless and isolated wanderer, will surely make us sympathise with him. When he dies, a uniquely powerful, individual force has been lost.

ELIZABETH-JANE

Elizabeth-Jane is described as 'our poor only heroine' (Chapter 43, p. 303). Many critics feel that Hardy encourages us to feel close to Susan's daughter through his use of her as a commentator, and because of the predominantly positive attitude displayed towards her by the narrator. The final paragraphs of the novel, which focus on the heroine and her world view – said to resemble Hardy's – provide an epilogue. By this point it seems appropriate that *The Mayor of Casterbridge* should close with Newson's daughter because she has proved her worth and strength many times. There is no more fitting advocate for the idea that life, which has indeed proved to be a drama mostly consisting of pain in this book, must carry on.

Hardy utilises Elizabeth-Jane's point of view many times to comment and reflect on characters, settings and events; in fact, she introduces us to Casterbridge life, first as she approaches the town in Chapter 3 and then when she makes her visit to Henchard in Chapter 9. Through her role as onlooker Elizabeth-Jane achieves wisdom, good judgement and an understanding of the vicissitudes of human existence. Elizabeth-Jane is the most balanced character in the book. Like Lucetta Elizabeth-Jane shares some characteristics of a Hardy 'type': she is the melancholy maiden buffeted by fate and circumstances. Besides the role of commentator and observer, Elizabeth-Jane performs a range of other functions. She provides a point of comparison with the other female characters. She is adviser, confidante and judge, most obviously when she lives with Lucetta, but Elizabeth-Jane also attempts to advise Henchard, for whom she eventually plays the role of carer. She relieves Henchard's suffering, becoming the object of and inspiration for a powerful love, which enables Henchard to grow and look beyond himself. Some critics suggest that she is a Cinderella figure. She is also the moral centre of the book, although the narrator is ambivalent about her

Victorian obsession with respectability, which can seem 'almost vicious' (Chapter 30, p. 213).

Elizabeth-Jane's roles and experiences suggest that we should find her sympathetic. From the moment she first appears, holding her frail mother's hand, she is reliable. We admire her acceptance that she must work for her keep, and applaud her lonely attempts to improve herself; in this novel Elizabeth-Jane is the only character who cares about books, and we should view this as a sign of her worthiness. She becomes more sympathetic as she suffers in silence in Henchard's and Lucetta's houses. Her determination and stoicism mirror Henchard's. This girl may not be as exciting as the mysterious Lucetta, but she is certainly satisfactory, increasing in stature as she copes with a range of difficult situations. The Casterbridge townsfolk recognise her superior qualities, which is fitting since she proves to be a valuable member of the community (this fact is stressed on the final page of the novel). By the time she appears on her wedding day in a snowy white dress – a symbol of her moral as well as physical purity – we will feel that she has earned her right to some happiness. Unlike the other two female characters, she ultimately wins the genuine respect of the men and women in her life, as well as the reader.

When Hardy revised *The Mayor of Casterbridge* for book publication he made Elizabeth-Jane more sympathetic still in the final chapter. In the serial Elizabeth-Jane openly rejects Henchard when he calls to offer her a gift (a caged goldfinch) on her wedding day. This meeting is omitted in the first English book version; instead we are presented with a moving portrayal of Elizabeth-Jane's regret at not attempting to find her stepfather sooner. This is perhaps a more appropriate finale, given the fact that Hardy wishes to close his narrative in a way that encourages us to accept the heroine's world view. It can be argued that the revised ending makes Henchard's isolated death more affecting: he has never had a chance to explain himself. Elizabeth-Jane is important throughout the novel, but she is more prominent in the second half as Henchard learns to love her. This is proof of the positivity that we come to associate with Elizabeth-Jane.

DONALD FARFRAE

Our perceptions of Donald Farfrae change as we read the novel. The townsfolk's different views of him influence our responses, as do the narrator's descriptions and comments. Essentially, the gloss wears off. Initially the young Scot is a very attractive character: educated, generous, calm, fair and thoughtful. He is also impulsive, shown by his note to Henchard and decision to stay on in Casterbridge. His ability to integrate himself into the local community and lack of ostentation go in his favour, and following his performance in The King of Prussia Farfrae seems to be a sufficiently romantic figure to take on the role of suitor for Elizabeth-Jane. Early in the novel biblical references help us to see Farfrae in a positive light. He is compared to David, who replaced Saul (1 Samuel 17:42). This comparison gives a clear indication of how Farfrae's relationship with Henchard will develop; but in spite of the fact that the Scot is a reluctant adversary, his pre-eminence over Henchard ultimately makes him less sympathetic.

There are a number of other factors that contribute to the diminution of his 'wondrous charm' (Chapter 37, p. 265). His treatment of Elizabeth-Jane goes against Farfrae; he almost asks her to marry him and then retreats, knowing that he cannot afford to make a financially imprudent marriage. When he rises in the world he does not return to the girl he was first attracted to (some critics go so far as to say Elizabeth-Jane is sacrificed). Instead, he courts and weds Lucetta. Some see Farfrae's seduction by this devious female as a sign of weakness. Because the Scot is taken in by appearances we might be tempted to view him as shallow. We might also feel uncomfortable when we learn that he is content for Elizabeth-Jane to remain in the house after his marriage: this is insensitive. There are further examples of his insensitivity in the latter stages of the novel, although Farfrae remains fair and generous.

To begin with his business acumen and ambition go in Farfrae's favour; he makes improvements, stands up for the workforce (Whittle) and eventually becomes a popular employer himself. However, in the second half of the novel we begin to feel that while Farfrae's ways may be more efficient, but they are in some way less human; it is as if Hardy recognises the benefits that inventions like the seed-drill will bring, but regrets the passing of Henchard's 'rule of thumb'. There are two factors in particular that go against Farfrae. First, he is often unable to comprehend Henchard's character and occasionally treats his former employer in a patronising way, whereas Henchard looked on him as a brother. Secondly, after Lucetta's death Farfrae's reflections are rather cool; the narrator tells us 'it was inevitable that the insight, briskness, and rapidity of his nature should take him out of the dead blank which his loss threw about him. He could not but perceive that by the death of Lucetta he had exchanged a looming misery for a simple sorrow' (Chapter 42, p. 297). These words suggest that the Scot's mercantile leanings have taken over from his romantic impulses, and if we compare his reaction to a bereavement with Henchard's misery at the loss of Elizabeth-Jane, we might feel tempted to criticise Farfrae. By this time we have also come to realise the futility of social ambition; Farfrae's acceptance of the position of mayor shows him putting public pride before private feeling, and we know how disastrous this has been in Henchard's life: throughout the novel Hardy insists on the emotional void that comes with worldly success. We might feel that the fact that he follows in Henchard's footsteps so exactly goes against Farfrae. It is hard not to feel that it is cruel that he gains Henchard's business, employees, 'fiancée', house, furniture and social position, all in a remarkably short time.

But if Henchard's character is fate, so is Farfrae's and his virtues and good sense never desert him. Even after the skimmington ride his desire for revenge against its perpetrators is short lived. Throughout, the Scot is used to show us Henchard's faults and act as a contrast. Farfrae's career enables Hardy to show us another example of the wheel of fortune in action; although we suspect Farfrae will be hard to push off his perch at the end: he is too rational and careful to indulge in the grand gestures that lead to Henchard's ruin. Ultimately we know that Elizabeth will be content and safe in his hands. But the young, fair Scot lacks the titanic, heroic qualities of his former employer, whose demise is powerfully affecting in a way that Farfrae's deeds and fortunes never are.

LUCETTA

In her cherry-red dress Lucetta would not be out of place in a Victorian **melodrama**. There are a number of similar female characters – vain, shallow, compromised – in Hardy's fiction. Lucetta is involved in – and ultimately the victim of – some of the more sensational episodes in *The Mayor of Casterbridge*. She is an ambivalent figure who becomes increasingly sympathetic as she suffers and the modern reader will probably pity her more than the novel's early readers, for whom the young Jersey woman would have been a scandalous female. Like Henchard Lucetta is impulsive, but her impetuosity is tempered by a more calculating self-interest. Almost immediately, she displays cunning and determination. Her treatment of Elizabeth-Jane and Henchard is often selfish, and Lucetta can also be accused of deceptive artificiality. Her flightiness stems from an unpromising beginning in life; Hardy seems to suggest that Lucetta is partly the victim of heredity. But Elizabeth-Jane is also the victim of difficult circumstances, and if we compare the two principal females, Lucetta is undoubtedly lacking in seriousness, strength and moral worthiness. It seems clear that the narrator – like the urban chorus – is unimpressed by her sophistication. Unlike the other strangers who settle in Casterbridge, Lucetta never really becomes part of or contributes to the community and after her death she is forgotten quickly. Even her husband understands that he has not suffered a great loss. In spite of this, and the fact that she is portrayed as a pursuer and seducer of men, Lucetta commands a good deal of sympathy. Like Susan, she is in a state of fairly constant anxiety for much of the novel, most particularly after her marriage. Her overwhelming desire for security, and the fact that she attains it so shortly before her death, makes her a rather tragic figure. Lucetta is frequently humiliated: by her past, by Henchard, by the bull, by the skimmington ride; it seems that she receives no respite. Part of this is undoubtedly her own fault for being changeable and secretive, but circumstances also conspire against her. We might also sympathise with Lucetta because it is clear that she feels very attached to and dependant on Donald Farfrae; she wishes to be a good wife and works hard to please him. As her looks fade she comes to seem increasingly powerless. Like Susan, we might feel tempted to say she is the victim of the men she encounters and tries to wring happiness from.

SUSAN

Susan is a victim who is presented with few choices. She appears to be cowed by her circumstances from the very first pages, when the narrator comments on her stoicism. The least developed of the three female characters, she remains a shadowy figure, who is appropriately nicknamed 'The Ghost' by the inhabitants of Casterbridge. Susan is understandably anxious much of the time: at the auction, during her brief sojourn at The King of Prussia, throughout her remarriage to Henchard. She is ailing and in decline from the moment she reappears in Chapter 3. In spite of this she displays determination on a number of occasions and is a good judge of character. She flings her ring at her husband after the auction with some spirit, '"Mike," she said, "I've lived with thee a couple of years and had nothing but temper! Now I'm no more to you; I'll try my luck elsewhere. 'Twill be better for me and the child, both."' (Chapter 1, p. 13). Later Susan persuades her daughter not to take Henchard's name. Her (some would say) cunning secrecy is driven by an understanding of her difficult husband and the instincts of a good mother; Susan knows how Henchard will react when he discovers Elizabeth-Jane is Newson's daughter and she wishes to improve her child's chances in life. This is shown when she sends anonymous notes to Elizabeth-Jane and Farfrae. Susan's letter writing is important to the plot; her badly sealed missive suggests that she wishes to tell the truth but fears the consequences, a pattern that is repeated elsewhere in the novel. She deserves the moving epitaph provided by Mother Cuxsom; she has been a selfless, long-suffering presence. Her naïveté and superstition also help us to sympathise with Susan.

RICHARD NEWSON

Newson's character is not fully developed, but he plays an important role and provides a point of comparison with Henchard. Like the principal characters he is a stranger to Casterbridge, who wanders in and participates – rather casually – in the action at key moments. This might suggest that he is a passive character, but Newson's habit of materialising mysteriously plays an important part in Henchard's destruction. On two occasions when he appears he is heard before he is seen; at the door of the tent at Weydon-Priors fair and then when he turns up in Mixen Lane at night. This makes his arrival more dramatic. We might feel that in spite of his generous character, Newson is a figure who represents destruction; his purchase of Susan and reclamation of Elizabeth-Jane are both actions that deal a body blow to Henchard, who is unable to survive the sailor's final return. Newson causes the **protagonist** insufferable anxiety. We might also feel that he is implicated – unintentionally – in Lucetta's death since he contributes money for the skimmington ride. Although he is affectionate to his daughter, we might feel that his love for Elizabeth-Jane does not compare with Henchard's. However, it is clear that Newson means no harm. He buys Susan because he feels she will be happier with him and then disappears when he knows it will be a kindness to her. He also shoulders some of the blame for the wife sale and excuses Henchard's lies. At Elizabeth-Jane's wedding – our final view of Newson – the sailor exuberantly joins in with the dancing, suggesting his warm geniality.

THE URBAN CHORUS

In his earlier Wessex novels Hardy had made use of a chorus of rustics, whose role it was to add information and provide humour and colour. These characters comment on the action and enable the author to establish and develop a sense of community. Some critics suggest that they add to the **realism** of Hardy's work. In *The Mayor of Casterbridge* the chorus of urban citizens performs the same functions, although a number of minor characters also serve a darker purpose. Essentially, the urban chorus can be divided into two social groups: the more 'respectable' and kind-hearted element (Longways, Coney, Whittle), many of whom frequent The King of Prussia, and the less savoury crowd who are associated with Saint Peter's Finger and Mixen Lane. These characters – Mother Cuxsom, Nance Mockridge and Charl – are not entirely wicked, but their desire to humiliate their social superiors has far-reaching consequences. Their deceit following the skimmington ride mirrors the deceptions of Henchard's life. Some critics have argued that this group, which includes the furmity woman and Jopp, acts out of a desire for class revenge. The chorus are present at all the major social events that take place and demonstrate their own philosophy.

Hardy shows us old customs, beliefs and ways of life through his use of the urban chorus. The minor characters appear at important moments when there are events of emotional significance; for example, the wife sale, Henchard's remarriage, Susan's death, Henchard's death. Some of their comments undermine or satirise the action (the discussion after the Henchard–Susan marriage) but on other occasions the urban chorus adds to the **pathos** of an event: notably Mother Cuxsom's epitaph for Susan, with its biblical cadences, and Whittle's account of Henchard's final days. Social gossip plays a significant role in this novel, again suggesting the importance of the urban chorus. And it is interesting that the more lowly members of Casterbridge society recognise Elizabeth-Jane's virtues before her social peers. These characters are integral to a full understanding of *The Mayor of Casterbridge*.

Members of this chorus are individualised and have specific functions in the plot. JOPP is the closest to a straightforward villain, although Hardy provides him with adequate motives for revenge against both Henchard and Farfrae: he is repeatedly snubbed. We cannot blame him for the skimmington ride: he meets Nance and Mother Cuxsom by chance, and the bundle of letters is not properly sealed. Jopp's degeneration – from manager to denizen of Mixen Lane – might also serve as a parallel to the disgraced mayor's career. Both men spiral downwards.

In contrast to Jopp, ABEL WHITTLE – also humiliated by Henchard – is a generous man, who never considers revenge. The clash over Whittle's treatment is a turning point; after this Henchard's relationship with Farfrae deteriorates rapidly. In the final chapter Whittle assumes a role akin to the Fool's function on the heath in *King Lear*; he selflessly cares for the broken, isolated Henchard, reminding us of his positive qualities.

THE FURMITY WOMAN makes four significant appearances in the novel, two of which have dramatic consequences. She is a catalyst at Weydon-Priors fair, providing Henchard with the alcohol that spurs him on to sell his wife. In the courtroom her revelation of the auction destroys the former mayor's character and social standing. It is appropriate that she makes her final destructive appearance in Mixen Lane when the skimmington ride is planned. Her own degeneration – she struggles to keep her business going – mirrors Henchard's fall and allows us to see the social consequences of economic decline in rural Wessex.

SOLOMON LONGWAYS and CHRISTOPHER CONEY provide another perspective on events and characters and we gradually come to trust their judgement; especially when they express doubts about the skimmington ride and comment on Elizabeth-Jane's superiority.

MOTHER CUXSOM provides a moving tribute to Susan when she dies and is more kindly than her neighbour NANCE MOCKRIDGE, who maliciously suggests the skimmington ride.

THEMES

THE INDIVIDUAL AND THE COMMUNITY

Hardy created a uniquely detailed portrait of rural life in his fiction. Most of his major novels are set in Wessex. He drew his inspiration from Dorset, the county of his birth and many of the locations in *The Mayor of Casterbridge* are modelled on Dorchester and its landmarks. We see all aspects of the Casterbridge community in this novel and social distinctions are important. Our first glimpse of the town comes in Chapter 4 as Susan and Elizabeth-Jane approach it on foot. Elizabeth-Jane observes that Casterbridge is 'an old-fashioned place', 'shut in by a square wall of trees, like a plot of garden ground by a box-ending' (Chapter 4, p. 27). This description suggests a tight-knit community. The narrator confirms Elizabeth-Jane's impression of 'this antiquated borough', which, we are told, is 'untouched by the faintest sprinkle of modernism' (Chapter 4, p. 27). We are being prepared for the clash that will take place between the old and the new when Henchard and Farfrae become rivals.

Throughout this chapter the town's proximity to and reliance on the surrounding countryside is emphasised. Hardy offers a long list of 'objects displayed in shop-windows' (Chapter 5, p. 28) to introduce the idea of commerce, which is to play an important role in the novel. It could be argued that this theme has already been introduced: the Weydon-Priors fair and the wife sale have already demonstrated the impact of trade on the personal life of the **protagonist**, as well as

introducing us to one of the old rural customs of the locality. The
prologue suggests that life in rural communities can be brutal, an idea
that will be developed later. Hardy will go on to describe the turbulent
histories of all the principal locations in Casterbridge: the Ring, the
bridges, the market-place and Mixen Lane are all associated with acts of
violence.

In succeeding chapters we learn that there are social divisions in
Casterbridge, and that business is precarious. Again, it could be argued
that the first chapter, in which Henchard sought work as a hay-trusser,
provided an introduction to these ideas. In Chapter 5 the querulous tone
Henchard displayed in Chapter 1 is echoed by the citizen who challenges
him about the 'bad bread' (p. 36). The lower classes and 'respectable
shopkeepers' (Chapter 6, p. 37) observe the feast being held at The
Golden Crown for 'the gentle-people and such like leading folk' (Chapter
5, p. 32) with a mixture of wonder and envy. It is clear from the
disgruntled townsman's interruption that the quality of the harvest affects
everybody and that the least powerful citizens are not afraid to make their
voices heard. Henchard is forced to act; he hires a manager to help him
improve his wheat. Later on he is bankrupted because he gambles on rain
at harvest time. In contrast, Farfrae succeeds because he brings innovative
farming and business methods to Casterbridge, which benefit the
community. He also endears himself to the populace because he is a fair
and congenial employer. The Scot's meteoric rise suggests that
Casterbridge will welcome helpful strangers; it also indicates that Farfrae
has successfully integrated himself into the life of the town.

Henchard is unable to do this with lasting success. Like Farfrae, he
was an outsider before he worked his way up from hay-trusser to corn-
factor. He has also created a thriving business. However, do we ever really
feel that he is part of the Casterbridge community? He seems to be an
isolated individual from the moment we see him through the windows of
The Golden Crown. At the banquet he is the only man whose glass is
never filled with grog; instead he 'drank large quantities of water'
(Chapter 5, p. 34). Chapters set in the inns in Casterbridge provide us
with an insight into the lives and opinions of the town's inhabitants. That
Henchard abstains, unlike almost every other character in the novel,
singles him out. The reader knows that he has deliberately chosen
temperance: the mayor makes himself an outsider. When he does start

drinking again, Henchard remains isolated. In Chapter 33 it is clear that he makes the respectable drinkers in The King of Prussia nervous when he forces the choir to sing Psalm 109, disturbing their weekly ritual. After they have taken 'their half pint regulation' (Chapter 33, p. 232) they move away from Henchard, who is led out of the inn by the long-suffering Elizabeth-Jane. By this point the young woman has become a respected figure in the town; here she shows appreciation of its values, as well as a desire to keep her stepfather out of trouble. The final chapters of the novel confirm Henchard's isolation from the community. Whittle follows him as he wanders into self-imposed exile, reminding us that his former employer possesses a sense of duty even if he cannot conform when he describes Henchard's kindness to his mother. This 'kind-like' behaviour (Chapter 45, p. 320) was typical of the protagonist. Giving Whittle's mother coal was an individualistic gesture, echoed by Henchard's magnanimous distribution of food to the poor after his celebration was wrecked in Chapter 16. These acts are the expressions of a singular personality who does not 'fit in'. We might feel that it is unlikely that Henchard was ever going to conform after selling his wife in the first chapter, although the novel does suggest, particularly in the evocation of Mixen Lane and its inhabitants, that anarchic acts and impulses are part of Casterbridge life.

What conclusions are to be drawn about the individual and his relationship with the community in The Mayor of Casterbridge? Does Hardy suggest that Henchard becomes a failure because he cannot – or will not – 'fit in'? Does the protagonist's individualism contribute to his downfall? Like the townsfolk, the narrator is ambivalent about Henchard's actions and character. Having taken Farfrae to their hearts, the people of Casterbridge then decide, when he prospers, that they feel more sympathy for the disgraced mayor; as the narrator tells us, 'he [Farfrae] had lost in the eyes of the poorer inhabitants something of that wondrous charm which he had had for them as a light-hearted penniless young man' (Chapter 37, p. 265). At the end of the novel we understand that we are supposed to value Elizabeth-Jane's selfless 'teaching' of the town's 'narrow-lived ones' (Chapter 45, p. 322). Henchard was never satisfied with simply contributing to the community. He wanted more. There was an emotional void in his life as mayor that he attempted to fill first with Farfrae, then with Lucetta, then with his stepdaughter. Is

Hardy perhaps celebrating his tragic hero's egotism at the end of the novel? His vehement and bitter will commands respect and Henchard's lonely death provides a sense of emotional **closure** that overshadows the muted final paragraphs about Elizabeth-Jane. It may be desirable and preferable to live as part of a community in this novel, but it is the unconventional Henchard who captures and holds the reader's imagination. Because he has focused with so much intensity on one man's struggle with himself, Hardy has succeeded in creating a powerful legend about perverse individualism.

LOVE, MARRIAGE AND COMMERCE

It is **ironic** that Farfrae should be seized on as a romantic hero by the female characters when his adversary is a much more passionate man. Henchard has little success in love because he habitually conducts his personal relationships with women as if they were business transactions. It is only after he is 'feminised' by his fight with Farfrae that he achieves any emotional satisfaction, and this is short lived because of his impulsive lies. Many critics have commented on the lack of real romance in this novel, which is dominated by commercial combat.

From the opening chapter when Henchard subverts the institution of marriage by selling his wife to another man, we can see that trade has a destructive effect on personal relationships. The protagonist struggles to reconcile his commercial instinct with his strong emotions and the results are disastrous. Descriptions of Henchard's early dealings with Susan, Lucetta and Elizabeth-Jane share the same ominous mercantile tone. He courts Susan with 'a business-like determination' and a 'dogged unflinching spirit, which did credit to his conscientiousness' (Chapter 13, p. 79). The second phrase is **ironic**; surely 'did credit' (a business term) negates Henchard's 'conscientiousness'? Later in Chapter 21 when the mayor wishes to rid himself of Elizabeth-Jane, who does not 'belong' to him (she is another man's daughter) he offers her money when she announces that she would like to leave his house:

> 'It had better be done properly,' he added, after a pause. 'A small annuity is what I should like you to have – so as to be independent of me – and so that I may be independent of you. Would that please ye?' (p. 140)

Henchard talks as if he were striking a bargain with a business partner, not like a man discussing his stepdaughter's future welfare. Shortly after this transaction is completed Henchard decides he 'must put' Lucetta 'in her proper position' by marrying her (Chapter 32, p. 145). The narrator suggests that this desire to order his emotional affairs is a 'mechanical transfer of his sentiments' following his estrangement from Elizabeth and Farfrae (Chapter 32, p. 147). It becomes clear that Henchard will gain nothing from these relationships because of his arid approach. He considers his own needs, concerns and expectations first, paying little attention to the feelings of the female characters.

Ironically, Henchard achieves limited emotional fulfilment through his paternal love for Elizabeth-Jane, in spite of the fact that she is unrelated to him by blood. He clings to her because she is worthy, but we might be tempted to feel that his loneliness is a driving force; all his other business and personal relationships have failed. Integral to his contentment with Elizabeth is the daily running of the seed shop, which his stepdaughter rules. Even here, commerce plays its part. Henchard is as possessive of Elizabeth as he was overbearing with Farfrae, whom he looked on as a brother. His relationship with the Scot suggests that it is dangerous to allow emotional impulses to govern business interests, just as it is unwise to conduct one's private life as if it were a commercial enterprise. However, Henchard has learned that possessiveness kills affection and attempts to control his jealous impulse to destroy Elizabeth's romance with Farfrae. He still views marriage suspiciously though: so far as Henchard is concerned, Elizabeth's union with Farfrae represents robbery (see Chapter 42).

If Henchard is a bad example of a husband (his union with Susan affords neither party much joy), the other unions that we see in the novel do not provide a much more promising or optimistic picture of male-female relationships. The most romantic moments are fleeting. Elizabeth-Jane and Farfrae enjoy a brief, rather awkward flirtation early on, which culminates in a hinted proposal. Farfrae then abandons the 'pleasing, thrifty and satisfactory' Elizabeth for the more dramatic charms of Lucetta (Chapter 15, p. 94). Was Farfrae ever a true romantic though? During their rendezvous at Dummerford barn in Chapter 14 he says to Elizabeth-Jane '… it's a great pity to waste out time like this, and so much to be done' (Chapter 14, p. 92). His attitude to his first love, displayed here and in the words quoted from Chapter 15, do not suggest a passionate man. Like Henchard, Farfrae is a businessman first. Perhaps Hardy wishes to undermine conventional notions of romance with his portrayal of Farfrae; his swift wooing of and marriage to Lucetta could be classed as a whirlwind romance, but we know that this relationship is built on deception. After her death Farfrae reflects on his first marriage pragmatically, and his tone echoes Henchard's mercantile musings about Lucetta (see Chapter 42). We are forced to conclude that Farfrae is an unsatisfactory lover too.

What of the *femme fatale*? Lucetta's life is dominated by her preoccupation with getting married. She moves to Casterbridge in pursuit of Henchard and then casts him aside when she meets a more attractive prospect. The narrator emphasises Lucetta's desire for security; it seems that even the woman who is driven by romantic impulses is looking for 'the best deal' she can find. When Henchard confronts her in Chapter 29 she says, 'I could not risk myself in your hands; it would have been letting myself down to take your name after such a scandal. But I knew I should lose Donald if I did not secure him at once ...' (Chapter 29, p. 209). Her words emphasise the importance of social standing, and suggest her desperate need to 'secure' the man who will offer her the best chance of happiness. After her secret wedding Lucetta seems to be a weak creature, who clings to her husband for dear life. The thought that her precarious security might be destroyed by the revelation of her previous 'bargain' with Henchard eventually kills her. It is ironic that the woman who dashes Henchard's final hopes of romance is herself brought down.

Elizabeth-Jane's romantic career seems to suggest the importance of compromising in love, just as Farfrae's business success points to the need for careful planning rather than impulsive gestures. Elizabeth-Jane survives the disappointment she must feel as she watches Donald fall in love with Lucetta and later accepts her faulty lover with good grace. Hardy does not suggest that Farfrae's second courtship of Elizabeth-Jane is at all romantic; he focuses on the anxiety it causes in Henchard. On the final page we are told that 'the lively and sparkling emotions' the heroine felt in her early married life 'cohered into an equable serenity' (Chapter 45, p. 322). Elizabeth-Jane's temperament has led her to this serenity; the more tempestuous Henchard never achieves this level of satisfaction.

We are forced to conclude that love is as hazardous as trade in *The Mayor of Casterbridge*.

FATE, CHANCE AND CHARACTER

Although Hardy explicitly links Henchard's fate to his character in Chapter 17 the text hints that the protagonist is not entirely responsible for his downfall. Chance meetings determine events too. Many commentators have criticised Hardy's supposedly heavy-handed use of coincidence, but it provides a powerful sense that there are cosmic forces operating beyond man's control. In *The Mayor of Casterbridge* the fetishistic Henchard certainly believes that there are supernatural powers working against him. Gradually, the reader is likely to become convinced of this too, although it is impossible to blame 'the powers above us' (Chapter 34, p. 240) for 'the momentum' of Henchard's character (Chapter 27, p. 190), which pushes him relentlessly towards catastrophe.

Let us consider some of the coincidences that help to determine the hero's fate. Newson's appearance in the tent doorway in Chapter 1 transforms the auction from sport to serious business. Although it is Henchard's belligerent nature that has led to the sale, Newson will later accept some of the blame for the destruction of his marriage. In Chapter 41 he says to Henchard, 'We were young and thoughtless' (p. 287). Interestingly, Hardy allows the protagonist to offer his own excuse, 'I was not in my senses, and a man's senses are himself' (Chapter 41, p. 287). Even allowing for the influence of alcohol, we will probably not find this explanation sufficiently convincing. All Newson's appearances after the first chapter prove disastrous for Henchard, who tells mad lies to protect his relationship with Elizabeth-Jane. Other characters who play important roles in Henchard's life appear as if by chance at significant moments. Farfrae happens to be passing through Casterbridge just as the mayor has advertised for a manager, Susan comes to 'reclaim' him just as he has reached the height of his success, Lucetta's arrival coincides with his wife's death. Elizabeth-Jane's relationship with her stepfather is ruined by chance; her mother fails to seal the letter revealing her paternity.

It seems to be Henchard's fate to suffer the consequences of the weather. His national holiday entertainment is ruined because it rains, then he gambles on bad weather at harvest time and loses heavily. This convinces Henchard that 'events are combined to undo him' (Chapter 31, p. 216). **Ironically**, the water preserves his life when he considers suicide. He stares into the river in Chapter 41 and sees the effigy of himself from the skimmington ride and decides that this is an omen that he must live. Again he feels that his life is being controlled by cosmic forces: '... it seems that even I am in Somebody's hand!' he declares gloomily (Chapter 41, p. 295).

However, the reader is most likely to feel that Henchard conspires against himself. His conflicting impulses lead to conflicts with others. He chooses to engage in 'mortal commercial combat' with Farfrae, he treats Elizabeth-Jane and Lucetta cruelly, he tells Newson heinous lies. We will probably feel that it is just that his evil impulses work against him. We might even agree with commentators who suggest Henchard's violations of society's rules and codes of conduct bring about retribution. This is an integral part of Hardy's conception of the way in which a man's character determines his fate. Youthful misdemeanours come back to haunt the characters in this novel: they cannot escape themselves or their pasts. This is perhaps why Farfrae succeeds; he has nothing to hide. Some critics have suggested that Henchard suffers too much as he expiates his sins. Perhaps this is also part of Hardy's tragic vision and Henchard's destiny; the protagonist is energetic in his destruction of others, so it is appropriate that he punishes himself with equal ferocity. Hardy may also be suggesting that it is man's lot to suffer and endure the hazards of fate and the impulses of one's own character, but this struggle leads to a perverse kind of heroism and nobility in this novel. As Henchard bitterly says – and proves – as he exiles himself, 'my punishment is *not* greater than I can bear!' (Chapter 43, p. 307). His will is a testament to his monumental determination and perversity.

SECRECY AND DECEPTION

The Mayor of Casterbridge is full of secrets and their revelation is always destructive. The prologue sets up the first secret, which dominates the lives of the principal characters until it is dramatically revealed in court by the furmity woman. This initial deception leads to further deceitful behaviour: the fake courtship of Henchard and Susan and the hoodwinking of Elizabeth-Jane. Much of the deception is driven by a desire to preserve social standing and reputation. It could also be argued that deception leads to the furtive, anonymous notes Susan sends to Farfrae and Elizabeth. We discover that the anxious mother wishes to encourage a match between the two because she fears the revelation of another secret, Elizabeth's paternity. Private deceptions lead to public humiliation: the most devastating example of this is the skimmington ride (which is also planned in secret). Lucetta is unable to bear the shame of having her past conduct revealed, although Henchard survives the revelation of the wife sale. It is possible to argue, however, that he exiles himself because he cannot bear to have his deception of Newson revealed. Secrecy has worn him down, as it exhausted Lucetta.

An addiction to 'scribbling' (Chapter 22, p. 146) is dangerous, as Susan's badly sealed letter suggests. Mrs Henchard is the only character who carries her secrets to the grave with her, although her constant anxiety suggests that secrecy and deception take their toll. Lucetta's career demonstrates this too. The fear of revelation makes her a victim, signified by the description of her in Chapter 35 as 'very small deer to hunt' (p. 248). Farfrae is drawn into furtive behaviour by Lucetta when the couple go to Port Bredy to wed in secret. The reader will realise that this is not an auspicious start to the marriage. When he discovers that she has married another man Henchard is devastated, 'idiotised' (Chapter 29, p. 209). Elizabeth-Jane's secret, that she loves Donald, is only maintained for Lucetta. The decision to keep silent about her affection helps her to keep her dignity, and avoids destructive rivalry with her companion. We might be tempted to feel that all the secrets in the novel were better kept, as this secret is, but Hardy insists that it is impossible to conceal scandalous actions or behaviour. Our conclusion must be that deception leads to public and private tragedy.

STRUCTURE AND NARRATIVE TECHNIQUES

Robert C. Schweik ('Character and Fate in *The Mayor of Casterbridge*', 1966) suggests that there are *four movements* in the novel, each opening on a relatively optimistic note and concluding with the destruction of hope. He argues that our perceptions of Henchard shift as his expectations decrease in each phase. In the first fourteen chapters the **protagonist** reaches the pinnacle of success, despite his actions in the opening chapter. But in Chapter 15 he clashes with Farfrae, and is seized by 'dim dread' (p. 100). A new cycle begins, ending with the furmity woman's revelation and Henchard's 'fall' (Chapter 31, p. 218). The disgraced mayor recovers briefly, but returns to drinking and is thrown into 'a state of bitter anxiety and contrition' (Chapter 40, p. 281) by his fight with Farfrae. In the final phase of the novel his precarious happiness is destroyed by Newson's return and Farfrae and Elizabeth's courtship. This leads to Henchard's self-imposed exile and death in Chapters 44–5.

Schweik's analysis suggests the importance of *repetition* in this novel. The phases described indicate that Hardy wished to create an impression of relentless and unavoidable decline. Within each phase the author also makes use of *mirroring*, which helps us to understand the roles that fate, chance and time play in the lives of the characters. Events are often mirrored by succeeding incidents; for example, Susan's journey with Elizabeth-Jane in Chapters 3 and 4 mirrors the journey in the **prologue**, highlighting the difference between her relationship with her daughter and Henchard's attitude to his family eighteen years previously. Henchard's meeting with Lucetta at the Ring in Chapter 35 recalls his earlier rendezvous with Susan in Chapter 11: the remorse he felt at that first clandestine meeting leads him to treat Lucetta kindly when he sees her standing in the same spot. At his lowest ebb Henchard thinks about emigrating, just as Farfrae considered seeking his fortune in a new country before he accepted the job of manager. The skimmington ride is an **ironic** parody of the royal visit and also reminds us of the banquet in The Golden Crown. These three public 'entertainments' demonstrate how far Henchard has fallen. The most important and extended example of mirroring is Farfrae's career, which replicates Henchard's. The Scot's rise coincides with his employer's fall, suggesting that the novel is structured to show a powerful example of the reversal of fortune. We will feel that man is struggling with forces beyond his control.

It is also clear from Schweik's analysis that Hardy has arranged his plot so that there is an *intense focus* on Henchard, who dominates the reader's imagination. All the other characters have their own 'voices' and concerns, but our reactions to them are inextricably bound up in our responses to the protagonist. It could be argued that Hardy has constructed his novel to show that it is Henchard who gives the other characters life (we might also feel he then goes on to try to destroy those lives, succeeding only in destroying himself). Henchard marries, discards and then remarries Susan, who needs him to provide Elizabeth-Jane with security. His money helps Elizabeth-Jane to improve herself and she blossoms in his house. He offers Farfrae work, enabling him to remain in Casterbridge and start a successful career. Lucetta comes to the town in order to seek out the man who has promised to marry her. It is ironic that she then rejects Henchard in favour of his rival. We have been prepared for this rejection by Elizabeth-Jane and Farfrae. They demonstrate that they will not endure Henchard's temper; suggesting that they have the strength to make lives of their own. We might feel that Hardy structures his novel to show that the life-giver, because he is driven by selfish motives, experiences a loss of power. However, as he is degraded, Henchard's emotional power grows; the reader feels increasingly sympathetic towards him as he destroys himself.

The structure described above is clearly the structure of *tragedy*, reminiscent of Greek drama, in which a hero is brought down by a fatal flaw in his character. Critics have argued about Henchard's faults: is it his temper, his impetuosity or his monstrous ego that defeats him? Critics have suggested that the first two chapters can be seen as a prologue to the main action; in the opening chapter the seeds of destruction are sown. It can also be argued that the final chapter concludes with an **epilogue,** in which the author shows the resolution of the conflict he set up at the beginning and comments on the way life will proceed after the hero's demise. Hardy's use of *the urban chorus* is also reminiscent of Greek tragedy. The townsfolk comment on the action at key moments, giving us insight into the protagonist and his struggle. They help us to understand the other principal characters. In The King of Prussia the drinkers respond favourably to Farfrae's arrival, contrasting with the dissatisfaction displayed outside The Golden Crown. Already we know that Henchard's position can be threatened. The chorus offers an ironic and gloomy assessment of Henchard's marriage to Susan. The furmity woman is critical of the former mayor's right to judge her, and destroys him with her revelation; from this moment onwards the chorus plays a more active role in the plot: like the main characters the townsfolk show that they have their own impulses, which must be taken into account. When Henchard scandalises the town during the visit of the royal personage, the chorus is there to witness his humiliation. The snubs that Lucetta receives on this occasion prepare us for the malicious skimmity-ride, which undermines the social standing of both those parodied. The fact that this event does not agonise Henchard as it destroys Lucetta suggests that the protagonist is moving beyond the reach of the chorus: gossip can harm him no more. Finally, Abel Whittle assists the isolated Henchard and describes his final journey and death; he is powerless to save his former employer, but his kindness is accepted.

Hardy employs other devices that point towards tragedy. *Chapter endings* frequently establish a sense of foreboding (for example, see Chapters 26, 34, 36, 42). This is partly because Hardy needed to leave his readers wanting more (the novel was originally published in weekly parts). Hardy also concludes his chapters with a moment of suspense that keeps the reader 'hooked'; the most masterly example of this is the end of Chapter 22, when Lucetta waits impatiently for Henchard to call. The chapter closes with a brief paragraph; the two, short, final sentences read: 'Lucetta flung back the curtain with a nervous greeting. The man before her was not Henchard' (p. 153). The reader recognises immediately that the protagonist's love affair with Lucetta is doomed, and anticipates further conflict.

Letters and overheard conversations point towards catastrophe and add to dramatic impact. Henchard's will can be seen as a companion to Susan's and Lucetta's fatal letters. The tragic protagonist's bitter pencilled words signify the end of his struggle. Deliberate or accidental eavesdropping causes anxiety in all those who hear a conversation not intended for their ears. When Henchard resorts to spying in Chapter 43 his telescope reveals that Newson has returned to Casterbridge. This discovery causes 'dark despair' (p. 304), adding to the misery he felt in the previous chapter when he learned, through his 'watchfulness', (p. 301) that Farfrae and Elizabeth were courting. *Chance meetings and arrivals* are often troublesome, and not just for Henchard. Elizabeth's hopes of a successful outcome to her romance with Donald are destroyed when Lucetta appears in Casterbridge, and the latter is undone as a result of Jopp's chance meeting with Nance Mockridge and Mother Cuxsom in Chapter 36.

The *contrasts* Hardy draws between characters and the *doubling* that Keith Wilson (editor of the current Penguin Classics edition) has identified, are an important part of Hardy's conception of structure. Susan, Lucetta and Elizabeth-Jane are very different, but their relationships with Henchard follow a similar pattern; initial attraction (we assume Henchard married Susan because he was gripped by youthful passion), followed by disillusionment and rejection, at which point the protagonist realises he has made a mistake and tries to make up for his cruelty. We see Henchard's moral and emotional progress in his relationships with these women; that he clings to Elizabeth-Jane and fully recognises her worthiness goes in his favour. But the fact that he repeats his mistakes in each relationship suggests a tragic outcome. There is the same *doubling* in the male characters; Henchard, Newson and Farfrae can be compared. By comparing Henchard with Newson and Farfrae we can see the protagonist's faults as a lover and a father, although Hardy does not present Newson and Farfrae as idealised figures.

Hardy makes use of **foreshadowing** and *omens*. The weather and settings reflect and anticipate events. In the first chapter the depressing scene (the dusty road, the rather dismal fair) hints that the Henchard marriage is all but over even before the auction. When Henchard meets Susan at the Ring in Chapter 11 we know that their reconciliation will afford neither much pleasure and lead to further strife because the setting is ominous; the narrator tells us that its 'associations had about them something sinister' (p. 69), going on to describe the amphitheatre's violent history, which includes being the site of the town gallows. Mixen Lane is a particularly sinister location (see also Textual Analysis, Text 2). The weather, too, portends disaster. In Chapter 16 Henchard's project for the national celebration is 'doomed to end in failure' because of the 'monotonous smiting of the earth by heaven in torrents to which no end could be prognosticated' (p. 102). The elaborate, biblical cadences of this description signify that more than an entertainment is at stake. Shortly after this Henchard's relationship with Farfrae breaks down. Henchard is again struck a fatal blow by the elements in Chapter 27, when there are 'three days of excellent weather' (p. 189). Hardy's repeated biblical and literary references to doomed characters (Job, Faust, Bellerophon) foreshadow the hero's ruin. These references are an example of *authorial intervention*; Hardy occasionally steps in to comment on Henchard's progress in order to prepare us for the tragic outcome. Settings are not simply portentous. The detailed descriptions of landscapes, streets and houses provide the reader with a feeling of **verisimilitude** and **realism,** which draws us in so that we feel we are observing a unique tragedy. At the same time the author wishes us to understand that we are observing something universal and inevitable; the violent history of the Casterbridge settings suggests that destruction is an unavoidable part of life, which occurs again and again. Hardy's use of **flashbacks** to provide information about his characters' pasts and motivations is another device designed to convince the reader that he or she is observing fully rounded, plausible characters.

Different narrative points of view inform our understanding of events and provide a balanced feeling to the novel as a whole. The **omniscient narrator** offers an overview, introducing us to key locations and characters. Often, as in the opening chapter, Hardy's technique is to begin the narration at a distance, establishing the characters in a setting, then moving in to observe them more closely. This technique is repeated many times; for example, when Henchard meets Susan at the Ring or when Jopp goes to Saint Peter's Finger with Lucetta's letters. Hardy adopts the same technique when he writes from a character's point of view. Elizabeth-Jane is used to provide the reader with an initial impression of Casterbridge. Thereafter we observe many events through her eyes, most poignantly the progress of Lucetta's love affair with Farfrae. It is appropriate that her view of Casterbridge life is employed: she is to become a reliable member of the community and the novel will close with this sober young woman. Elizabeth-Jane's hard-won detachment contrasts vividly with Henchard's passion and adds to the feeling of balance. Often the story is told from the narrator's and a character's viewpoint almost simultaneously; this enables Hardy to give the reader a feeling that he or she is particularly close to the actions and feelings of the characters. An example of this occurs at the end of Chapter 40, when Henchard calls to find out how Lucetta is progressing after her epileptic fit:

> Henchard regarded the sympathetic speaker [Elizabeth-Jane] for a few instants as
> if she struck him in a new light; then, without further remark, went out of the
> door and onward to his lonely cottage. So much for man's rivalry, he thought.

Death was to have the oyster, and Farfrae and himself the shells. But about Elizabeth-Jane; in the midst of the gloom she seemed to him as a pin-point of light ... She was not his own; yet, for the first time, he had a faint dream that he might get to like her as his own – if she would only continue to love him (Chapter 40, p. 283)

The sentences are constructed to create the impression that we are following Henchard's train of thought, as well as being given information about his movements by the narrator. At times Hardy switches almost seamlessly between different points of view (see Chapter 24 and Textual Analysis, Text 1), a technique that again provides the reader with a feeling of proximity to the action. Altogether, Hardy's narrative techniques make *The Mayor of Casterbridge* psychologically and emotionally convincing. The extensive use of *dialogue* to convey feelings and ideas helps to draw the reader in; Hardy prefers to allow his characters to 'speak' in their own words, although reported speech is also used. Like the flashbacks and narrative points of view, dialogue creates the impression of verisimilitude or realism.

LANGUAGE, DESCRIPTION AND STYLE

Hardy has been accused of writing in an affected and exaggerated style, which relies too heavily on clumsy **metaphors**. His use of biblical and literary references has come under fire, as has his use of recondite vocabulary. However, he has also been praised for the simplicity, poetry and grace of his prose. The modern reader will find examples of over-elaborate phrasing in this novel (you might feel that the description of the bad weather that ruins Henchard's entertainment, quoted in Structure and Narrative Techniques, is over-elaborate), and the use of dialect vocabulary and biblical and literary allusions may seem to hinder full understanding, but these aspects of Hardy's style do not detract from its power. It must also be remembered that the Victorian reader would have been more familiar with the classical references Hardy makes, and with the Latin phraseology that inhibits some readers. Critics have argued that the – to some – intrusive use of quotations and literary references is an integral part of Hardy's exploration of the importance of the past and history in *The Mayor of Casterbridge*.

Much of the power of the novel is attributed to the detailed descriptions of settings and characters; this is a very *visual* book. Hardy plays close attention to what his people are wearing. Clothes are not just expressions of character, they also define social position, and are often **symbolic.** When he first appears Henchard is dressed in 'a short jacket of brown corduroy, newer than the remainder of his suit, which was a fustian waistcoat with white horn buttons, breeches of the same, tanned leggings, and a straw hat overlaid with black glazed canvas' (Chapter 1, p. 3). The narrator goes on to describe the tools of his trade that Henchard is carrying; overall the impression is of a skilled working man who has fallen on hard times. When we next see him Henchard's dramatic rise is signified by the expensive and impressive clothes he wears: 'an old-fashioned evening suit, an expanse of frilled shirt showing on his broad chest; jewelled studs and a heavy gold chain' (Chapter 5, p. 33). These items, especially the gold chain, symbolise the mayor's power. In the first phase of his decline Henchard continues to wear the 'old blue cloth suit of his gentlemanly times, a rusty silk hat, and a once black satin stock, soiled and shabby', suggesting that he is struggling to accept his diminished status, but at the end of the novel he puts on 'the working clothes of his young manhood, discarding forever the shabby genteel suit of cloth and rusty silk hat' (Chapter 43, p. 306). We know that with his return to hay-trusser's garb the protagonist has accepted his fate.

The clothes that Elizabeth-Jane and Lucetta wear are important too. Elizabeth flirts briefly with fashion, but is uncomfortable when she realises she is setting herself up as 'the town beauty' (Chapter 15, p. 94). When she leaves Lucetta's house after her companion has married Farfrae she 'takes off her pretty dress and arrays herself in a plain one' (Chapter 30, p. 215). This recalls her arrival in Casterbridge, when she was wearing simple black mourning clothes. Despite the simplicity of her dress, her worthiness and charm become apparent to the people of Casterbridge, who are not ultimately impressed by Lucetta's expensive gowns. Lucetta takes clothes very seriously, perhaps signifying her superficiality and flightiness. She finds it difficult to choose a new dress: 'settling upon new clothes is so trying ... You are that person ... or you are *that* totally different person ... for the whole of the coming spring' (Chapter 24, pp. 165–6). Eventually she determines to keep a cherry-red gown: a symbol of her dramatic, attention-seeking personality.

Hardy makes use of natural imagery when evoking characters and settings. Henchard is often compared to big cats: his affection for Farfrae is 'tigerish' (Chapter 14, p. 88). Later in the novel he becomes 'a netted lion' and 'a fangless lion' (Chapter 42, p. 297, Chapter 43, p. 303), signifying his loss of power and status. We are invited to draw comparisons between human and animal behaviour at the start of the novel. In Chapter 1 Henchard's cruel treatment of his wife occurs yards from 'the sight of several horses crossing their necks and rubbing each other lovingly' (p. 14). The sale of 'a very promising brood mare' precedes the auction (p. 9). There are unpleasant images that hint at the destruction to come; in the furmity tent there is a man with 'eyes like buttonholes' and 'a damp voice'.

The language Hardy uses to describe Casterbridge and Mixen Lane provide the reader with clear visual images of the contrasting locations: the former is 'a sturdy plant', while the latter is 'a mildewed leaf' (Chapter 36, p. 252). These metaphors neatly encapsulate the characters of these settings. Elsewhere in the novel Hardy conveys the beauty of Casterbridge, as well as its agricultural and business life. The attractiveness of the town comes across as Elizabeth-Jane makes her way to Henchard's house in Chapter 9. She sees 'through tunnels, the mossy gardens at the back, glowing with nasturtiums, fuchsias, scarlet geraniums, "bloody warriors", snapdragons and dahlias, this floral blaze being backed by crusted grey stone-work remaining from yet a remoter Casterbridge than the one visible in the street' (p. 59). The life and colour suggested by this precise description reveal Hardy's appreciation of nature and Elizabeth's youth and current optimism: the reader can see that she will blossom in this town. This is an example of what Raymond Chapman (*The Language of Thomas Hardy*, 1990) identifies as Hardy's genius for making human moods concrete through imagery. This is also an example of Hardy's listing technique, which he uses to give the reader a strong visual impression of a setting – adding to the realism of the novel. Descriptions of settings are also poetic, a good example being of Casterbridge:

> Bees and butterflies in the corn-fields at the top of the town, who desired to get to the meads at the bottom, took no circuitous course, but flew straight down the High street without any apparent consciousness that they were traversing strange

latitudes. And in autumn airy spheres of thistledown floated into the same street, lodged upon the shop-fronts, blew into drains; and innumerable tawny and yellow leaves skimmed along the pavement, and stole through people's doorways into their passages with a hesitating scratch on the floor, like the skirts of timid visitors. (Chapter 9, pp. 56–7)

The **personification** of the insects and leaves is particularly effective; it brings the scene to life and creates an impression of town and nature coexisting harmoniously and almost indivisible one from another. **Alliteration** and **simile** add to the poetical quality of the description.

Reported speech is not used as extensively as *dialogue*. Characters speak with their own 'voices' and idioms. Their contrasting styles and modes of speech highlight the differences between the varying social groups and individuals in Casterbridge society. Henchard's speech is often energetic and pithy; he uses oaths and colloquialisms as well as standard English, and *dialect* which conveys his old-fashioned ways and down-to-earth approach. However, in Chapter 20 he takes Elizabeth-Jane to task for her 'occasional pretty and picturesque use of dialect words' (p. 127), reprimanding her in a characteristically forceful manner, 'Good G–, are you only fit to carry wash to a pig-trough, that ye use such words as those?' (p. 127). This example is not only **ironic**, it points to the tensions and contradictions within Henchard; he uses dialect himself but feels his stepdaughter's style undermines his prestige. We can also see whose side the author is on: Hardy values and respects dialect. The ultimate expression of the mayor's direct and powerful style is his will, a list of stark requests.

Lucetta's melodramatic nature comes across in many of her utterances and letters. In Chapter 39 she watches the skimmington ride with increasing agitation, '"It is of no use!" she shrieked out. "He will see it, won't he? Donald will see it. He is just coming home – and it will break his heart – he will never love me any more – and oh, it will kill me – kill me!"' (Chapter 39, p. 275). Her confusion and agony are neatly conveyed by the short words and phrases and repetition. Farfrae's Scots dialect signifies that he is an outsider, but also conveys his romantic charm, as does his singing. Hardy's use of dialect elsewhere, in descriptive passages and scenes involving the urban chorus, is extremely effective in establishing the character and customs of the rural way of life, and helps him to locate his story in place and time, again adding to the novel's realism.

Although Hardy has been accused of over-elaborate sentence construction, he is also the master of dramatic simplicity. Short sentences are used effectively to convey tension. Lucetta's fit in Chapter 39 provides a fine example of this. The dialogue is crucial to the drama of this moment, but the punchy narrative adds to its impact:

> She stood motionless for one second – then fell heavily on the floor.
>
> Almost at the instant of her fall the rude music of the skimmington ride ceased.
>
> (pp. 275–6)

PART FOUR

TEXTUAL ANALYSIS

Lucetta and Elizabeth-Jane have gone out into the market place to take a closer look at the new horse-drill that has just arrived in Casterbridge. Here they meet Henchard and Farfrae (p. 167).

TEXT 1   (FROM CHAPTER 24)

Among all the agriculturists gathering around, the only appropriate possessor of the new machine seemed to be Lucetta, because she alone rivalled it in colour.

They examined it curiously; observing the rows of trumpet-shaped tubes one within the other, the little scoops, like revolving salt-spoons, which tossed the seed into the upper ends of the tubes that conducted it into the ground; till somebody said 'Good morning, Elizabeth-Jane.' She looked up, and there was her stepfather.

His greeting had been somewhat dry and thunderous, and Elizabeth-Jane, embarrassed out of her equanimity, stammered at random, 'This is the lady I live with, father – Miss Templeman.'

Henchard put his hand to his hat, which he brought down with a great wave till it met his body at the knee. Miss Templeman bowed. 'I am happy to become acquainted with you, Mr. Henchard,' she said. 'This is a curious machine.'

'Yes,' Henchard replied; and he proceeded to explain it, and still more forcibly, ridicule it.

'Who brought it here?' said Lucetta.

'Oh, don't ask me, ma'am!' said Henchard. 'The only thing – why 'tis impossible it should act. 'Twas brought here by one of our machinists on the recommendation of a jumped-up jackanapes of a fellow who thinks –' His eye caught Elizabeth-Jane's imploring face, and he stopped, probably thinking that the suit might be progressing.

He turned to go away. Then something seemed to occur which his stepdaughter fancied must really be a hallucination of hers. A murmur apparently came from Henchard's lips in which she detected the words, 'You refused to see me!' reproachfully addressed to Lucetta. She could not believe that they had been uttered by her stepfather; unless, indeed, they might have been spoken to one of the yellow-gaitered farmers near them. Yet Lucetta seemed silent; and then all thought of the incident was dissipated by the humming of a song, which sounded as though from the interior of the machine. Henchard had by this time vanished into the market-house, and both women glanced towards the corn-drill. They could see behind it the bent back of a man who was pushing his head into the internal works to master their simple secrets. The hummed song went on:

'Ta-s on a s-m-r aftern-n

A wee bef-re the s-n w-nt d-n,

When Kitty wi' a braw n-w g-wn

C-me ow're the h-lls to Gowrie.'

Elizabeth-Jane had apprehended the singer in a moment, and looked guilty of she did not know what. Lucetta next recognised him, and more mistress of herself, said archly, '"The 'Lass of Gowrie" from inside of a seed-drill – what a phenomenon!'

Satisfied at last with his investigation, the young man stood upright, and met their eyes across the summit.

'We are looking at the wonderful new drill,' Miss Templeman said. 'But practically it is a stupid thing – is it not?' she added, on the strength of Henchard's information.

'Stupid? Oh, no!' said Farfrae, gravely. 'It will revolutionize sowing hereabout. No more sowers flinging about their seed broadcast, so that some falls by the wayside, and some among the thorns, and all that. Each grain will go straight to its intended place, and nowhere else at all!'

'Then the romance of the sower is gone forever,' observed Elizabeth-Jane, who felt herself at one with Farfrae in Bible-reading at least.

This is an important moment in the text: the four characters who will dominate the second half of the novel are gathered together in one location. This is the first time Henchard has met Lucetta since her arrival in Casterbridge and the first encounter Elizabeth has had with her stepfather since leaving his house. Significantly, this meeting occurs in public in the market place, the focus of activity in the town and a consistently important location in the novel. It is an appropriate meeting place: *The Mayor of Casterbridge* focuses on a man whose life is wrecked by the public revelation of a prior misdemeanour and his intense commercial and personal rivalry with his former business manager. Throughout this extract the public and private are linked; the dialogue and narration both make this explicit.

In spite of the fact that we see the characters in a public place of commerce, it is clear from the narration that private concerns are uppermost in the characters' minds, with the possible exception of Farfrae (this is appropriate: unlike Henchard, the young Scot is able to separate his personal feelings from his business concerns most of the time). Henchard is stung that Lucetta has refused to see him, as we can tell from Elizabeth-Jane's puzzled 'hallucination'; and Lucetta and Elizabeth-Jane have been drawn outside because they wish to see Farfrae, to whom they are both attracted. The narrator emphasises the different ways in which the two women conduct themselves as they interact with the male characters. Elizabeth-Jane is uncomfortable with Henchard – shown by her embarrassed stammering – and she has to content herself with silent observations about Farfrae. Her behaviour follows on logically from what has gone before and what will occur shortly. Prior to this chapter the girl endured cruel treatment in Henchard's house, and in the next chapter she will continue to suffer because of Farfrae, who now ignores the young woman he almost proposed to. His preference for Lucetta is hinted at in the song that he sings here, about a girl in 'a braw n-w g-wn'.

Lucetta is more assertive than her overlooked companion. We do not know how – or if – she responds to Henchard's murmured reproach ('she seemed silent'); this phrase maintains suspense and prepares us for Lucetta's later decision not to know Henchard in public. From her polite and formal greeting it seems clear that she is not disconcerted by meeting the man with whom she has enjoyed a secret liaison, despite the fact that she has now transferred her attentions elsewhere. At this point in the novel it certainly seems as if Lucetta is playing the role of *femme fatale* with some success; the narrator's use of the adverb 'archly' suggests this, as does the fact that she is quickly 'mistress of herself' when she realises that the man on the other side of the horse-drill is her new beau. Lucetta's arresting cherry-red dress, which makes her the 'only appropriate possessor' of the machine hints that she has already won Farfrae and suggests her melodramatic nature, which becomes more apparent later on. However, the narrator hints that the Scotchman will make the wrong match when he marries Lucetta; Elizabeth-Jane is 'at one with Farfrae in Bible-reading', and it is clear that the entrepreneur is a businessman before he is a romantic hero, despite his fondness for singing. When we first see him here he is attempting to master the 'simple secrets' of the drill and is concerned that 'Each grain will go to its intended place'. As the final chapters makes plain: Farfrae's correct place is by the serious and equally hard-working Elizabeth's side. In the second half of the novel the mercantile part of Farfrae's nature is developed further.

As for Henchard; he is associated with old agricultural methods, shown by his ridiculing of the seed-drill. This public criticism of innovative farming methods, clearly associated with Farfrae, is an example of the jealousy his former manager now excites in him. Here the men are presented as rivals in love and business. By his standards, Henchard is relatively restrained in this extract, probably because he is in a public place. This shows his sensitivity to social niceties, which fits in with his respectable courtship and remarriage of Susan earlier. Henchard does possess some sense of decorum, although we might feel he finds formality unnatural and restricting. Certainly he moves off quickly: the narrator informs us that he 'vanished into the market house'. Does his swift exit suggest that he is uncomfortable, annoyed, more at home with business than affairs of the heart? Returning to what little he does say, we might feel that Henchard cuts himself off because he does not wish to cause Elizabeth-Jane distress; ironically he believes that she is being courted by his unwitting and as yet unidentified rival, Farfrae. This hint of feeling for a fellow creature fits in with the regret he showed at the end of Chapter 21 when she left his house, and might also be taken as a sign that his relationship with Elizabeth-Jane will improve later. However, we cannot even be sure of this much generosity. The ambivalent tone that is often adopted by the narrator when describing the protagonist is signified by the use of the word 'probably': we cannot be sure why Henchard stops speaking. This word is also used to add to the mystery that is being set up (remember, Lucetta 'seemed silent'). We might be tempted to believe that Henchard is considering his own feelings most in this extract; the narrator reports his actions and thoughts in language that reflects Henchard's viewpoint when we learn he believed that 'the suit might be progressing'. These cool, calculating words suggest that Henchard views his own and others' relationships as business transactions; the reader will remember that he wished Farfrae to marry Elizabeth-Jane because it would get her off his hands. And in spite of his restraint, there are indications that Henchard remains volatile and alarming. He speaks to Elizabeth-Jane in a 'dry and thunderous' tone, his exaggerated bow, made with 'a great wave' of his hat suggests his physical power, and his direct, forceful, colloquial description of Farfrae as 'a jumped-up jackanapes of a fellow' hints at the intensity of his growing hatred. Added to this, his murmured reproach might seem dangerous and indiscreet, but, as we are already aware, the impetuous mayor can never avoid expressing his feelings, particularly when he is wounded. We may feel that his reproach is not entirely justified; the mayor deliberately held off calling on Lucetta until it suited him and this perversity has already cost him dear: Lucetta is no longer his for the asking. However, we will feel for Henchard – and Elizabeth-Jane. The latter regrets the loss of 'the romance of the sower', a view that we become sympathetic with as Henchard is destroyed and displaced by Farfrae and his new methods. At the end of the novel Henchard returns to hay-trussing, while the triumphant Donald takes his place as mayor and chief employer in the town. Although Hardy suggests that new innovations are exciting and beneficial (the neat and effective, visual description of the drill at the beginning of this extract makes clear the machine's fascination), his emotional sympathy seems to lie here – as elsewhere – with Henchard and his rule of thumb.

Hardy's narrative techniques in this extract are typical of the novel as a whole. He makes effective use of situational **irony**. It is highly ironic – and dramatic – that the unwitting rivals in love and business should be in such close proximity without seeing or speaking to one another. It is also ironic that Henchard believes Farfrae loves his overlooked stepdaughter when we know he has already succumbed to Lucetta's charms, and cruelly ironic that he should reproach Miss Templeman in a manner typical of a wounded lover when she no longer cares for him. The narrator gently mocks Farfrae in a way that has become familiar when he says the young man 'was pushing his head into the internal works to master their simple secrets'. To everyone else the machine is anything but simple: is the narrator undermining Farfrae's assumed superiority? Is he trying to make the young man look slightly ridiculous, singing with his head in a machine while his lover stands nearby? Since we associate him with the machine, does the fact that Lucetta's dress 'rivalled it in colour' undermine Farfrae as a lover, or is this sentence intended as a swipe at Lucetta, who has set herself up as a dazzling mystery, rather like the machine? Interestingly, there also seems to be some playful mockery in the rather bold words Lucetta's uses to gain her lover's attention ('what a phenomenon!').

We do not just hear from the **omniscient narrator** here. Hardy seamlessly works in his characters' points of view, as we have seen from the Henchard example above. By using the characters Hardy is able to add drama and offer other compelling perspectives on events. Elizabeth-Jane, who is often cast in the role of the observer and whose judgement we have come to trust, reacts to Henchard's reproach. We can picture the girl's puzzled amazement as she looks at 'the yellow-gaitered farmers', trying to ascertain whether or not she is hallucinating. Her point of view enables Hardy to leave some of the details of this moment enigmatic: the reader has to decide what has happened from the evidence provided. Suspense is maintained because Elizabeth-Jane 'detected' the murmured words as if she were a spy. Hardy also introduces Henchard and Farfrae in a way that suggests Elizabeth-Jane's point of view. In each case their sudden arrival on the scene causes her consternation. It is a favourite technique of Hardy to introduce characters through aural details in *The Mayor of Casterbridge*, increasing the impact of their appearances. Appropriately, given their status as rivals, Henchard and Farfrae are both heard before they are seen, although their utterances could not be more different. Henchard's arrival is dramatic, as befits the man of ungovernable passions; a long sentence describing the drill closes with 'till somebody said "Good morning, Elizabeth-Jane." She stood up and there was her stepfather.' This thunderous greeting contrasts with the pleasant 'humming of a song' by Farfrae, which dissipates all thoughts of his rival. Hardy's use of dialogue encourages us to compare the two men, as the narration encourages us to compare Elizabeth-Jane and Lucetta. Henchard is polite but rather explosive ('Oh, don't ask me, ma'am!') while Farfrae speaks 'gravely' with measured biblical cadences when discussing the merits of seed-drill. Hardy rarely uses reported speech, preferring that his characters reveal themselves in their own words, making his writing more vivid and immediate, and giving his reader the impression of being close to the action. The use of characters to relate or comment on incidents has the same effect.

Another of Hardy's favourite techniques is the chance meeting. Here it seems that the characters are drawn simultaneously to the seed-drill (and by implication Farfrae), but their arrival on the scene at the same moment is coincidental. This pattern is repeated throughout the novel, in which the timing of events and revelations is crucial. The recurring theme of deception, so common in Hardy's novels, is evident in this extract. Henchard and Lucetta are both trying to protect their secret shared past, which Henchard almost gives away when he reproaches Lucetta; the fact that he is on the verge of revelation at this very first meeting suggests that the truth cannot be concealed for ever. All the characters are being deceived at this point in the novel and each has his or her own secrets. Ironically, Henchard knows least; he assumes Lucetta is still pursuing him and believes Farfrae loves his daughter. Elizabeth-Jane does not know the truth of her birth. Farfrae is unaware of Lucetta's past liaison and she does not know the truth of Henchard's first marriage. All these secrets must come out. Because this first meeting occurs in the market place, it seems likely that the characters will find themselves exposed publicly later in the novel. In this tense extract Hardy sows the seeds for further conflict.

TEXT 2   (FROM CHAPTER 36)

The narrator describes the most deprived area of Casterbridge, Mixen Lane (p. 252).

> The lane and its surrounding thicket of thatched cottages stretched out like a spit
> into the moist and misty lowland. Much that was sad, much that was low, some
> things that were shameful, could be seen in Mixen Lane. Vice ran freely in and out
> certain of the doors of the neighbourhood; recklessness dwelt under the roof with

the crooked chimney; shame in some bow-windows; theft (in times of privation) in the thatched and mud-walled houses by the sallows. Even slaughter had not been altogether unknown here. In a block of cottages up an alley there might have been erected an altar to disease in years gone by. Such was Mixen Lane in the times when Henchard and Farfrae were mayors.

Yet this mildewed leaf in the sturdy and flourishing Casterbridge plant lay close to the open country: not a hundred yards from a row of noble elms, and commanding a view across the moor of airy uplands and corn-fields, and mansions of the great. A brook divided the moor from the tenements, and to outward view there was no way across it – no way to the houses but round by the road. But under every householder's stairs there was a mysterious plank nine inches wide; which plank was a secret bridge.

If you, as one of those refugee householders, came in from business after dark – and this was the business time here – you stealthily crossed the moor, approached the border of the aforesaid brook, and whistled opposite the house to which you belonged. A shape thereupon made its appearance on the other side bearing the bridge on one end against the sky; it was lowered; you crossed, and a hand helped you to land yourself, together with the pheasants and hares gathered from neighbouring manors. You sold them slily the next morning, and the day after you stood before the magistrates, with the eyes of all your sympathising neighbours concentrated on your back. You disappeared for a time: then you were again found quietly living in Mixen Lane.

Walking along the lane at dusk the stranger was struck by two or three peculiar features therein. One was an intermittent rumbling from the back premises of the inn half-way up; this meant a skittle alley. Another was the extensive prevalence of whistling in the various domiciles – a piped note of some kind coming from nearly every open door. Another was the frequency of white aprons over dingy gowns among the women around the doorways. A white apron is a suspicious vesture in situations where spotlessness is difficult; moreover, the industry and cleanliness which the white apron expressed were belied by the postures and gaits of the women who wore it – their knuckles being mostly on their hips (an attitude which lent them the aspect of two-handled mugs), and their shoulders against doorposts; while there was a curious alacrity in the turn of each honest woman's head upon her neck, and in the twirl of her honest eyes, at any noise resembling a masculine footfall along the lane.

Critics who wish to claim Hardy as a novelist of social protest might fix on his descriptions of Mixen Lane and its inhabitants as proof that he was concerned to expose the sufferings of the poor. This extract certainly indicates that life among the poorest sections of the Casterbridge community is harsh; people live with the threat of disease and are forced to poach and prostitute themselves in order to survive. However, Hardy does not moralise. Nor does he condemn the inhabitants of this dismal area, although he states unequivocally that Mixen Lane is the home of thieves and murderers, and **personifies** vice and recklessness in order to add to the impression of iniquity. It could be argued that the final sentence of the first paragraph suggests that Hardy wishes to point out that the inhabitants of Mixen Lane have been abandoned and are the victims of social exclusion (the two mayors we see are never concerned to improve their living conditions), but it is also possible to conclude that the author simply wishes to show that vice exists and must be tolerated, however regrettable this might be.

Hardy describes this important location with his customary skill and attention to detail. Personification – mentioned above – is one of the many devices the novelist uses to bring his settings to life. By this point in the novel we have a clear picture of the different streets, houses and inns that make up the town, and their inhabitants. The idea of community is central to *The Mayor of Casterbridge* and the novelist wishes us to see all facets of its life. Mixen Lane is the least attractive part of Casterbridge, but **ironically**, given the inhabitants' degradation, a very powerful place: the fatal skimmity-ride will be planned here. In order to prepare us for this event Hardy takes us on a 'tour' of the area, ending up (shortly after this extract) in Saint Peter's Finger, where Lucetta's letters will be read. Many critics have argued that Casterbridge is an important 'character' in this novel, and Mixen Lane clearly has a life – and customs – of its own.

To begin with we see the lane from a distance: the cottages stretch out 'like a spit' (an unattractive and threatening image); then we move closer to observe the roofs, bow-windows and 'crooked chimney' (an obvious hint of unpleasantness). In spite of the precision of the viewpoint the location seems in some ways anonymous: none of the people described in this extract is named. This is appropriate given the fact that the inhabitants are involved in nefarious dealings. In the second paragraph we are placed at a distance again and we realise that this setting of shame is ironically close to the 'mansions of the great'. The unhealthiness of Mixen Lane, which is compared to a 'mildewed leaf', is part of the 'sturdy and flourishing' plant which is Casterbridge, and feeds off it. This is made clear in the third paragraph when we discover that the poachers bring home 'the pheasants and hares gathered from neighbouring manors'. The denizens of Mixen Lane encroach on the lives of their betters by thieving, just as the skimmity-ride will have a dramatic impact on the new mayor's wife. These people cannot be contained.

Having offered an overview of the area Hardy then focuses on specific details. The description of the 'mysterious plank' which exists under every householder's stair draws us closer to the scene again, and we learn that Mixen Lane comes to life after dark. Just as the market-place is a bustling hive of activity in the daytime, Mixen Lane has its own 'business time', reiterating the commercial theme of the novel. The succeeding paragraphs reveal the night-time activities and haunts of the inhabitants, preparing us for the parade of effigies, which will also occur at night. Are we implicated in the goings-on that we observe? The narration places us in the scene: 'If you, as one of the refugee householders ...', 'You sold them slily ...', 'You disappeared for a time ...'. The use of second person is unusual in this novel and adds interest and immediacy to the writing; it also encourages the reader to imagine for herself what life here must be like. But at the same time it enables Hardy to maintain the careful, almost protective, anonymity mentioned above. A hint of sympathy is perhaps added with the description of neighbours watching one of their own being sentenced in court. It could also be argued that the use of the second person suggests inquisitive but cautious discretion (the narration takes us close to the action, but the formality and elegance of some of Hardy's phrasing: 'extensive prevalence', 'situations where spotlessness is difficult' suggests the reader, and the narrator, remain at a distance).

However, the narrator seems cautiously fascinated by the shadowy people and places described, as the paragraph about the owners of the 'suspicious' white aprons shows. Throughout the novel Hardy pays a good deal of attention to his characters' clothes; they give us information about the wearers' natures and social standing. So what do these incongruous aprons suggest about the women in Mixen Lane? How can they be so clean in this grubby area? Immediately, however, they become less savoury, almost threatening as they stand there with their 'knuckles being mostly on their hips'. We are not encouraged to view these prostitutes as attractive: they look like 'two-handled mugs' and they are self-evidently not 'honest' (the repetition of this word makes it ironic). It is also clear that appearances are deceptive: the white aprons barely conceal 'dingy gowns'. This detail is significant: it adds to our understanding of the central theme of deception and prepares us for the shaming of Lucetta, the woman for whom clothes are most important in this novel. The elegant female will shortly be parodied in an entertainment devised by Nance Mockridge and Mother Cuxsom, who no doubt wear the same 'dingy gowns' as these prostitutes.

As well as offering us arresting visual images of Mixen Lane, Hardy also describes the sounds that 'a stranger' (again, the language hints at distance) might hear when making his way through the streets. In contrast to the market place, Mixen Lane is oddly quiet, as suggested by the description of the released prisoner returning to live 'quietly' in the lane. This is ironic: the tremendous noise of the skimmity-ride will be heard all over Casterbridge. The quiet helps to establish the sense of unease that Hardy is building up. Even the sounds described are not inviting, just as the stealthy, curious movements of the poachers and prostitutes discourage us from lingering. In the third paragraph the habit of whistling on return from a poaching trip is described; the low sound indicates the importance of stealth and secrecy, intimating that these people have a lot in common with their so-called 'betters': Henchard has gone to great pains to conceal his youthful sins. Then there is the ominous 'rumbling' from the skittle alley and more whistling, the 'piped note of some kind coming from every door'. Finally we learn that the women are waiting for 'any noise resembling a masculine footfall along the lane'. The air of vagueness in these descriptions ('of *some* kind', 'any noise *resembling*') again indicates the shadowy nature of life in Mixen Lane and the night-time location, and maintains the sense of unease mentioned above. We also notice that there is an absence of colour in spite of the careful and detailed descriptions: apart from the suspicious aprons, the houses, lanes and surrounding area are devoid of colour. This again reinforces the darkness of the setting, but also hints that life has been drained out of the inhabitants of Mixen Lane.

However, we do not doubt that Mixen Lane is a force to be reckoned with. The personification of its vices suggests that the community has a wild life of its own which is the antithesis of life in High Street Hall, the market place, even The King of Prussia. It is appropriate that the degraded and villainous Jopp should end up here. The fact that life in Mixen Lane continues, in spite of cholera epidemics and imprisonment and regardless of the town's succession of mayors hints at the inhabitants' strength. Most importantly, like almost every other significant location in *The Mayor of Casterbridge*, Mixen Lane is associated with violence and death, specifically 'slaughter'. This dramatic noun, which implies lawlessness, is a dark omen. Hardy seems to be stressing the importance of the past when he refers to the murders of days gone by; as we already know, it is impossible to escape the past in this novel. Will Mixen Lane simply be living up to its reputation when it causes Lucetta's death? Finally, Hardy's technique of listing details when he describes a setting (see the third sentence in the first paragraph, the final sentence in the fourth paragraph) adds to our sense that Mixen Lane will struggle on. The long sentences move at a pace that suggests a kind of jaded vitality. Altogether, this is an absorbing but repellent and threatening introduction to Mixen Lane and the crowd who frequent Saint Peter's Finger. After reading this extract we know that trouble is brewing when Jopp accompanies Mother Cuxsom and Nance to the inn.

TEXT 3   (FROM CHAPTER 45)

Abel Whittle describes Henchard's last journey and death (p. 320).

'Not – dead?' faltered Elizabeth-Jane.

'Yes, ma'am, he's gone! He was kind-like to mother when she wer here below, sending her the best ship-coal, and hardly any ashes from it at all; and taties, and suchlike that were very needful to her. I couldn't forget him, and traipsed out there to look for him, about the time of your worshipful's wedding to the lady at yer side, and I seed him walking along in the rain, and I thought he looked low and faltering. And I followed en over the road, and he turned and saw me, and said

"You go back!" But I followed, and he turned again, and said, "Do you hear, sir? Go back!" But I saw that he was low, and I followed on still. Then 'a said, "Whittle, what do you follow me for when I've told you to go back all these times?" And I said, "Because, sir, I see things be bad with ye, and ye wer kind-like to mother if ye were rough to me, and I would fain be kind-like to you." Then he walked on like that all night; and in the blue o' the morning, when 'twas hardly day, I looked ahead o' me, and I seed that he wambled, and could hardly drag along. By that time we had got past here, but I had seen that this house was empty as I went by, and I got him to come back; and I took down the boards from the windows, and helped him inside. "What, Whittle," he said, "and can ye really be such a poor fond fool as to care for such a wretch as I!" He was as wet as a sponge, and he seemed to have been wet for days. Then I went on further, and some neighbourly woodmen lent me a bed, and a chair, and a few other traps, and we brought 'em here, and made him as comfortable as we could. But he didn't gain strength, for you see ma'am, he couldn't eat – no, no appetite at all – and he got weaker, and to-day he died. One of the neighbours have gone to get a man to measure him.'

'Dear me – is it so!' said Farfrae.

As for Elizabeth, she said nothing.

'Upon the head of his bed he pinned a piece of paper, with some writing upon it,' continued Abel Whittle. 'But not being a man of letters, I can't read writing; so I don't know what it is. I can get it and show ye.'

They stood in silence while he ran into the cottage; returning in a moment with a crumpled scrap of paper. On it there was pencilled as follows: -

'Michael Henchard's Will

'That Elizabeth-Jane Farfrae be not told of my death, or made to grieve on account of me.

'& that I be not bury'd in consecrated ground.
'& that no sexton be asked to toll the bell.
'& that nobody is wished to see my dead body.
'& that no murners walk behind me at my funeral.
'& that no flours be planted on my grave.
'& that no man remember me.

'To this I put my name.

'MICHAEL HENCHARD'

'What are we to do?' said Donald, when he had handed the paper to her.

She could not answer distinctly. 'Oh, Donald,' she said at last. 'What bitterness lies there! But there's no altering – so it must be.'

Abel Whittle's moving account of Henchard's death and Elizabeth-Jane's quiet acceptance of the terms of her stepfather's will provide us with a sense of **closure**. It seems appropriate that Whittle is the only witness to his disgraced former employer's demise. Henchard has deliberately isolated and punished himself, and here he is attended by a simple character who is as powerless socially as he has become. Like Henchard, who has returned to hay-trussing, Whittle lives off and works on the land. We understand that Henchard has returned to the natural world; he has chosen to die in an isolated rural spot and his final journey has taken him close to the scene that was described in the opening chapter when he made his way to Weydon-Priors with Susan. The wheel has come full circle. This idea is reinforced by Whittle's references to the past; he feels attached to Henchard because he was 'kind-like' to his mother and wishes to repay him. This quiet generosity and the kindness of the woodmen who provide 'a bed and a chair' is especially moving because Henchard, as a self-condemned 'wretch', does not expect kind treatment. It is also touching that the simple Whittle proves to be as determined as Henchard: he won't go back and his former master will be cared for whether he likes it or not. It is also **ironic** that Whittle, who said he could not bear the disgrace Henchard had subjected him to in Chapter 15, now accompanies the man who shamed him on his final journey. More ironic still, Henchard's sense of shame has prompted him to make this journey.

The use of Whittle as storyteller encourages us to see Henchard as a Lear figure. Like the Fool in Shakespeare's play, Whittle seeks to offset his former master's misery as he battles against the elements. Throughout this extract, which is full of pain, there is also a suggestion of human goodness and empathy, which is reinforced in the final paragraphs of the novel when Hardy stresses that Elizabeth-Jane will become a useful member of her community. We will also note that Whittle has 'chosen' Henchard over Farfrae: in spite of the fact that his new employer is a

more congenial man, Whittle finds himself doggedly loyal to his old
master. This is a clear indication that we are to sympathise with
Henchard. By this point in the novel we share Whittle's strange inability
to reject Henchard, in spite of his irascibility. Whittle's understated
sympathy mirrors ours and heightens the **pathos** of this scene.

Abel is not patronised, and there is none of the humour associated
with the urban chorus that was found earlier. Although his speech is
simple, it is eloquent and direct, and entirely appropriate to the events
related. On the first occasion that we saw Whittle he appeared to be a
slightly ridiculous figure as he was herded through Casterbridge without
his breeches. Now he is dignified. His humility and ability to forgive
former ill-treatment suggest his dignity. The fact that Hardy gives
Whittle a long speech – uninterrupted by his audience – adds to this
dignity. Whittle's use of dialect vocabulary ('wambled') and grammar
('seed', 'wer') individualises the speaker and reinforces the idea that
Henchard is dying as a country man. Some critics would suggest that the
use of a dialect speaker to report Henchard's death proves that Hardy
wished to show that the lower classes in Casterbridge are as worthy of
interest as their social superiors. Throughout this novel Hardy has used
dialect to add vitality and interest to his tale and to help establish his
Casterbridge community. One of the community's least regarded figures
now steps humbly into the spotlight. This is appropriate: as we have seen
from the skimmity-ride, the lower classes can and do impact on the lives
of their 'betters'.

Hardy suggests Whittle's simplicity through his almost childlike
sentence construction, using simple conjunctions, 'And', 'Then', 'But'.
The repetition of this simple construction adds to the pathos of
Henchard's death: there seems to be an inevitability about 'and then …
and then', which also evoke the gruelling nature of Henchard's final
journey. The idea that death is quietly accepted as a natural part of
life in *The Mayor of Casterbridge* is reinforced by the matter-of-fact tone
in which a neighbour goes to 'get a man to measure him [Henchard]'.
The vehemence of Henchard's will adds to the sense of closure. Hardy
works carefully to make Whittle's account a piece of oral storytelling,
suggesting rural customs. The account includes some of Henchard's own
words, which add immediacy and a feeling of intimacy that would be
lost if his death were reported by an **omniscient narrator**. Whittle's

account is characteristic of Hardy's strong visual style. The **simile** 'as wet as a sponge' gives us a clear picture of Henchard's suffering. The concentration on Henchard's movements ('faltering', 'wambled', 'drag along') has the same effect.

Whittle's descriptions suggest that Henchard dies very much as he lived: he is still strong-willed and contrary, even though he is 'faltering'. He yells at Whittle, 'You go back!', castigates himself and walks all night in his weakened state. We know that his end is near when he finally allows himself to be helped into the cottage. This empty, desolate, boarded-up dwelling is an appropriate place for Henchard to die: it reflects the emptiness and loneliness he feels. Does he will himself to die? He forces himself to walk on, and we might be tempted to think that his loss of appetite is a deliberate choice; in the previous chapter Henchard miserably noted that he couldn't die if he tried, suggesting how fervently he wished to be obliterated. Hardy links his death to Elizabeth-Jane's marriage in Whittle's account; the simple man comes across Henchard walking in the rain at 'about the time of your worshipful's wedding to the lady at yer side'. This suggests that his stepdaughter's acceptance of Farfrae is the final, unendurable rejection. It makes us feel that the Scot has triumphed at the expense of another man.

Henchard's will is both matter-of-fact and bitter; it is exactly what we would have expected from the tragic **protagonist** and in its forceful repetitions clearly suggests the power of the man. It seems to present the fulfilment of his destiny promised by earlier references to Faust and Bellerophon. Henchard's deep attachment to Elizabeth-Jane is clear; she is the first person mentioned in the will and in death her stepfather generously tells her not to grieve for him. Some might argue that this is a sign of Henchard's monstrous ego (the fact that he has written a will at all might suggest this); he still expects her to mourn him even though he has lied to her and Newson. Henchard's fetishism is shown when he asks not to be 'bury'd' in consecrated ground; he rejects society as he feels it has rejected him. Here he perhaps aligns himself with the forces of nature rather than man and religion; just as his earlier sale of his wife might be pointed to as the action a natural rebel who could not – and will not – conform. Henchard's grim determination to be forgotten seems as powerful as his earlier desire to make his way in the world and be noticed. Now he rejects the trappings of success. The bleakness of his death is reinforced by one small but sad detail: he does not even wish 'flours' to be planted on his grave; they of course, would be a sign of remembrance and affection. Has Henchard rejected humanity completely?

Elizabeth-Jane and Farfrae's reactions frame Henchard's death for the reader, and their different reactions to Whittle's account and the will are telling. Like her stepfather before his death, Elizabeth falters when she learns what has happened. Her silence is eloquent: she is clearly deeply moved. We have to imagine her regret. Her silence might also be seen as a mark of respect. When she does speak she shows empathy; she understands that Henchard's dying commands must be obeyed. It seems cruel that she is too late to forgive or be reconciled to Henchard, but this is in keeping with the tone and philosophy of the novel, throughout which timing has often been disastrous. Her 'so it must be' suggests finality, and shows that she accepts death stoically, in the same way that Henchard accepted it. Farfrae's incomprehension confirms the lack of understanding he has so often displayed towards Henchard: his question, 'What are we to do?' is impotent, pointless. At the end of this extract we share Elizabeth-Jane's regret and Whittle's sympathy, but we probably feel less well disposed towards Donald Farfrae, who will never inspire the intense feelings his former employer has evoked.

PART FIVE

BACKGROUND

THOMAS HARDY'S LIFE AND WORKS

Thomas Hardy was born on 2 June 1840 in Higher Bockhampton, a village near Dorchester in Dorset. He was the son of a builder and master mason; his mother, who suffered great hardship in her youth, had been in service before her marriage. At the time that he was born, in the early years of Victoria's reign, the agricultural revolution had already taken place. Dorset remained a fairly isolated county, one of the poorest in England, although there was increasing social mobility. When Hardy was seven the railway arrived in Dorchester.

Hardy's family were very much part of the local community: his father, grandfather and uncle were all part of the local choir, playing music in Stinsford church, and Hardy began his education in the village school. He was not, as some have suggested, a self-taught peasant. His mother had ambitions for her son, encouraging him to read, and he progressed from the village school to Dorchester High School. At sixteen Hardy was apprenticed to John Hicks, a local architect. He continued to study in his spare time, learning Greek and Latin. He also struck up friendships with people who encouraged him in his ambitious quest for knowledge, notably the family of the Reverend Henry Moule, the vicar of Fordington, and the local poet and teacher, William Barnes, whose dialect poetry was an important influence on him. By this point Hardy was leading his life in three worlds: the rural hamlet of his birth, the county town and his own world as a student.

When he completed his architect's training Hardy moved to London to pursue his career. He prospered at Arthur Blomfield's practice, but gradually lost interest in architecture, becoming more drawn to literature. He tried to get his poetry published, but was not successful. Hardy began to have religious doubts at this time. He was influenced by Darwin's *On the Origin of Species* (1859) and the works of other scientists and agnostics, including John Stuart Mill. Later he was attracted to the philosophy of Thomas Huxley, Arthur Schopenhauer and Matthew Arnold. Other literary figures he admired included Swinburne, Keats and Shelley.

In 1867 Hardy fell ill and moved back to Dorset to work with Hicks again. He was still struggling to establish himself in the literary world, writing, in 1868, his first unpublished novel, *The Poor Man and the Lady*, a social satire on the upper classes, which proved too extreme for publishers. Hardy had decided to pursue a career as a novelist because he felt that he had a better chance of making a living this way, rather than as a poet. His talent was recognised by the novelist George Meredith, who advised him to write a more conventional, closely plotted novel; *Desperate Remedies* (1871) was the result. It was published at Hardy's own expense. By this time Hardy was living in Weymouth, still working as an architect. During 1871 he met and fell in love with Emma Gifford, whom he had met while working on restoring St Juliot's Church in Cornwall. Emma was the daughter of the rector. They married in 1874, after the enormous critical and commercial success of *Far from the Madding Crowd* (1874). Emma was very supportive of Hardy's work and helped him with his novels. Prior to their marriage Hardy had written *Under the Greenwood Tree* (1872), praised for its attractive depiction of pastoral life, and *A Pair of Blue Eyes* (1873), which was partly autobiographical. These two novels attracted enough attention for Hardy to be asked to contribute a serial to the *Cornhill Magazine*; this commission led to *Far from the Madding Crowd*, which established Hardy – and Wessex – on the literary map.

The Hardys began married life in the West Country, spending three years in London before returning to Dorset in 1881, and moving to Dorchester in 1883. Renewed daily contact with his roots seems to have had a very positive effect on Hardy's work. During the years before his return to Dorchester Hardy wrote another satire (this time of London life), *The Hand of Ethelberta* (1876) and *The Return of the Native* (1878), a powerful depiction of life in a remote Wessex location, Egdon Heath. Back in Dorchester Hardy began work on *The Mayor of Casterbridge*, which was serialised in 1886. In 1885 the Hardys moved into Max Gate, a house that Hardy had designed himself. He was to live here until his death in 1928. He and Emma began to spend three months of each year in London during 'the season'; although Hardy remained ambivalent about the 'dinners and clubs and crushes' that were part of life in the capital. The couple also travelled abroad. Some critics and biographers have suggested that the more sombre mood of Hardy's later fiction was partly a reflection of his marital disappointment: he and Emma were not always happy together and had no children. But in spite of the fact that Hardy held unconventional ideas about love and marriage, believing that couples who were not temperamentally suited should not have to remain together, he stayed with Emma. Their estrangement appears to have started in 1892, and was worsened by Emma's unenthusiastic reception of *Jude The Obscure*. By 1898 the couple largely 'kept separate'.

Hardy's own favourite among his novels, *The Woodlanders*, was published in 1887, followed by two great tragic novels, *Tess of the d'Urbervilles* (1891) and *Jude the Obscure* (1895). *Tess* and *Jude* were criticised for their immorality, and the reception of *Jude* persuaded Hardy to abandon novel-writing altogether. Thereafter he concentrated on his first love, poetry. *Wessex Poems* appeared in 1898, and was followed by other collections, as well as *The Dynasts* (1903–8), Hardy's epic verse-play about the Napoleonic Wars. Hardy's poems were generally well received and his literary reputation and popularity continued to grow. In 1908 he rejected a knighthood, although he became a member of the Order of Merit in 1910. In the same year he also received local recognition for his achievements, being made a Freeman of Dorchester. Emma died in 1912. Her death affected Hardy profoundly; some of his finest poems were inspired by her passing. Two years later Hardy married Florence Dugdale, several years his junior. She had been working as his secretary for some time and was also the author of children's stories. In the final years of his life Hardy was visited by and corresponded with a number of other writers, including H.G. Wells, Virginia Woolf and Siegfried Sassoon. The outbreak of the First World War was deeply disturbing to Hardy, who had become disillusioned with 'civilisation'. During his last years Hardy also worked on his autobiography, which was published posthumously in Florence's name. He died on 11 January 1928. His ashes were buried in Poet's Corner in Westminster Abbey. His heart was buried in Emma's grave.

Hardy's other published novels are: *The Trumpet Major* (1880); *A Laodicean* (1881); *Two on a Tower* (1882); *The Well-Beloved* (1897 though written earlier). His collections of short stories were: *Wessex Tales* (1888); *A Group of Noble Dames* (1891); *Life's Little Ironies* (1894); and *A Changed Man and Other Tales* (1913). He also wrote essays, the best-known being 'The Dorsetshire Labourer', published in 1883 in

Longman's Magazine. It focuses on the working conditions suffered by 'the labouring poor' of his native county and includes the kind of social comment that informs his Wessex novels, especially *Tess*.

Historical background

The Mayor of Casterbridge is set in the years before the Repeal of the Corn Laws in 1846, laws which had imposed heavy duties on imported corn and intended to protect English farmers and merchants. Hardy deliberately chose this period because he wished to show the effects of uncertain harvests on the agricultural community and the way in which a harvest could lead to fortunes being made or lost; Henchard, whom some see as one of the last old-style profiteers, is ruined when he gambles on bad weather at harvest time. Although the Repeal of the Corn Laws encouraged wheat imports, change was not really apparent until the railways in North America were extensively developed, enabling wheat to be transported more easily. In spite of this, things were changing, even in Dorset, which was a remote and old-fashioned county at that time. Farmers and merchants were changing the ways in which they ran their businesses and new innovations were being introduced. These changes are reflected in the novel: Farfrae introduces new methods and is associated with new machines, while Henchard is most comfortable with his old-fashioned approach to trade, in spite of his initial enthusiastic reception of Farfrae.

At the time that Hardy was writing *The Mayor* Dorchester was still predominantly an agricultural town. Its reliance on agriculture is reflected in the novel: Casterbridge's economy depends on the harvests. The prologue shows Henchard moving across Wessex to find work, just as many labourers had to do in Dorset in the nineteenth century. Rural superstitions and customs continued to play an important part in the life of the community; there is evidence that conjuring and witchcraft were still believed in up until the 1890s. By the time that he was sixteen Hardy had witnessed two public hangings, and he would have been familiar with the hiring fairs that occur in the novel. The skimmington ride, the wife sale and Henchard's superstitious oath swearing and visit to the weather prophet are all inspired by the county of his birth. Critics and biographers have identified real-life examples of wife sales reported in *The Dorsetshire County Chronicle*, which Hardy read when he decided to write his 'historical novel'. His appreciation of the history and architecture of Dorchester comes across in many descriptive passages; particularly in his evocation of the Roman amphitheatre, the Ring. The visit of the royal personage that occurs in Chapter 37 was probably inspired by an occasion when Prince Albert passed through Dorchester on his way to Weymouth in 1849.

But Hardy was not merely concerned to evoke the folk memories and beliefs of Dorset; he also reflects some of the class consciousness of his age. He had thought long and hard about the plight of the labouring poor – Dorset's agricultural workers were among the poorest in the country – and his concerns led him to write with some sympathy about the social deprivation found in Mixen Lane, the home of prostitutes and poachers. Hardy also refers to the cholera epidemic that swept through the real life Mixen Lane. Abel Whittle's inability to read reflects the fact that Dorset workers were still largely uneducated. Successive education acts had changed things slightly, and would continue to do so, leading to depopulation, which was also the result of the changes in the economy and agricultural working methods. Hardy himself attended a school run by the National Society for Promoting the Education of the Poor in the Principles of the Established Church between 1848 and 1850, and he suffered feelings of inferiority throughout his life, in spite of the fact that he was 'upwardly mobile'. His father, though not a peasant (he employed six men), was not middle class. In *The Mayor of Casterbridge* class distinctions are clearly drawn; we see the great difference between life in High Street Hall and Mixen Lane. The bitterness of class relations is also explored briefly; Henchard is challenged about the 'bad bread', and the denizens of Mixen Lane exert their revenge on Lucetta in the skimmington ride. Although he does not show the harshest aspects of rural life during the period in which the novel is set, he does reveal the impact that changes and class attitudes had on people's lives.

The Mayor of Casterbridge also reflects some of the changes in moral values and attitudes that were taking place. Hardy began to have religious doubts when he was a young man; many others were beginning to question traditional Christian teaching and interpretations of the Bible.

Darwin's *Origin of the Species* had an enormous impact, as did the work of other agnostics, nonconformists and early feminists. In *The Mayor* Hardy seems to undermine the Christian belief in Providence, which held that there are benign forces operating in the world for man's benefit; Henchard believes in a malignant power controlling his fate, and he perhaps suffers more than he deserves to. We might feel that *The Mayor of Casterbridge* closes on a cautiously optimistic note (Elizabeth and Farfrae are content together and life goes on), but Hardy also suggests that man has to accept that life is 'a brief transit through a sorry world' and that 'happiness' is 'but the occasional episode in a general drama of pain'(Chapter 45, p. 322). Hardy's pessimism comes across more strongly in his later novels, particularly *Tess* and *Jude*.

It might also be argued that the novel offers us new models of male-female behaviour, although the happiest couple – Farfrae and Elizabeth – are undoubtedly conventional. Henchard's relationships with Susan and Lucetta are unorthodox, but Hardy does not condemn his characters as immoral.

LITERARY BACKGROUND

Strictly speaking, Hardy can be considered a Victorian novelist, although many critics have argued that he was not a typical Victorian. He read widely and worked hard to improve the perceived deficiencies in his style, turning to Fielding, Scott and Defoe for inspiration. Hardy also enjoyed the poetry of Swinburne and Tennyson, and references to their works can be found in his novels. References to Shakespeare and Milton also occur. At the time that Hardy was living in London and starting out on his own literary career Thackeray was the most eminent novelist of the day; his reputation was gradually eclipsed by that of George Eliot, whom Hardy considered a great thinker, but not a great storyteller. Ironically, when *Far from the Madding Crowd* was published, it was assumed that she was the author. Eliot is considered by many to be one of the foremost **realists**, who sought to represent the world as it was, rather than as it should be. Although Hardy is concerned with offering a realistic portrait of country life, the poetic and mythical aspects of his work suggest that he was not a realist in the way the term is understood today.

Hardy's novels can be linked to the work and aspirations of the Romantics: his rural characters often seem to speak in what Wordsworth referred to as 'the real language of men' (Preface, *Lyrical Ballads*, 1802), and his preoccupation with the natural environment was shared by many of his literary antecedents. However, Hardy's view of nature differed from the Romantics' and he rejected their idea of Providence. Books about rural life were very popular at the end of the nineteenth century, and Hardy had an early success with *Under the Greenwood Tree* (1872), which some critics feel presents a **pastoral** idyll. But Hardy also focused on some of the hardships faced by agricultural communities, most notably in *Tess* (1891), where the heroine is forced to wander across Wessex in her struggle to make a living from the land. Although he was perhaps occasionally guilty of patronising his rural chorus and using agricultural stereotypes, Hardy was attempting to show the importance of the local customs of country dwellers in Dorset. In 'The Dorsetshire Labourer' (1883) he criticised London attitudes to agricultural workers. His use of dialect has literary antecedents: the Dorset poet William Barnes wrote in dialect and a number of popular novels included dialect: Emily Brontë's *Wuthering Heights* (1847) and Eliot's *Adam Bede* (1859) are two examples.

Early in his career Hardy was advised to make his plots more cohesive by George Meredith. He looked to the highly popular sensation novels of the day, notably the melodramatic and suspenseful works of Wilkie Collins (*The Woman in White*, 1860, *The Moonstone*, 1868). Some of the more improbable incidents and coincidences in Hardy's fiction can probably be traced back to this genre, although Hardy rejected the form after he had little success with *Desperate Remedies* (1871). In *The Mayor of Casterbridge* the use of letters and overheard conversations can seem contrived.

Hardy's was a unique novelist in many ways. All his major novels are about ordinary people, foreshadowing the fiction and drama of the twentieth century. He was the first to place a series of novels in a particular location (apart from Trollope, whose intentions and concerns were very different from Hardy's) and the first to explore rural life in the kind of detail that other novelists were using to depict life in the industrialised towns. Although there are realistic and **naturalistic** elements in his work, he is more concerned to produce a poetic impression of life – what he called 'a series of seemings'. Hardy is not a moraliser, nor is he a didactic novelist. He did not wish to force a 'message' on his readers. The ambivalence of his narration often suggests this, as does his eschewing of traditional happy endings. In Hardy's novels characters do not always learn through suffering or receive what they deserve. Hardy rejected orthodox Christianity, as Henchard does in his will. He was accused of being morbid, radical and pessimistic, and immoral in his depiction of male-female relationships. These aspects of his work, and his philosophical beliefs, suggest that Hardy was a man of the twentieth rather than the nineteenth century. But there are paradoxes in his oeuvre. At times Hardy's novels evoke nostalgia for a bygone age, and his reverential descriptions of customs and folklore suggest that there is a conservative impulse in his work. Undoubtedly Hardy disliked some aspects of change and it is interesting to note in his fiction that those who transgress are punished. These contradictions are demonstrated in *The Mayor of Casterbridge*: the moderniser Farfrae triumphs but Hardy's emotional sympathy undoubtedly lies with the old-fashioned Henchard.

PART SIX

CRITICAL HISTORY AND BROADER PERSPECTIVES

EARLY RECEPTION

By 1886 Hardy was a well-known author, and he could expect *The Mayor of Casterbridge* to be widely reviewed. Its reception was mixed, as was the case with most of his fiction. Some reviewers felt that *The Mayor* was disappointing; a number disliked the novel's pessimism and objected to the lack of gentrified characters (publishers almost turned down the novel because of the lack of gentry). Others felt that the characters and situations were improbable. Hardy himself felt that 'it is not improbabilities of incident but improbabilities of character that matter'. More positive commentators admired Hardy's depiction of his urban chorus and his use of dialect, although there were some critics who felt that dialect was used inconsistently and was therefore unsatisfying. Hardy's use of exaggerated similes and metaphors also attracted criticism. *The Spectator* reviewer did not appreciate Hardy's 'pagan reflections', although he did praise some aspects of Henchard's characterisation. *The Athenaeum* suggested that the novel proved that Hardy 'has a wonderful knowledge of the minds of men and women', especially the less educated classes. An American reviewer, writing in 1892, felt that Henchard was 'a remarkable character-study from the point of view of a psychologist or sociologist' but went on to add 'that does not make him a proper hero for a novel'. Overall Hardy was disappointed by the book's reception, noting fatalistically 'I have not, however, expected any great praise of the book; I know its faults too well.'

Early reviews and comments on these reviews can be found in the following books:

R.P. Draper, ed., *Hardy: The Tragic Novels*, Macmillan Casebook, 1983
    Includes extracts from Hardy's autobiography, *The Life of Thomas Hardy* and 'The Dorsetshire Labourer' and two essays on *The Mayor of Casterbridge*, as well as some early comments on his fiction

Ray Evans, *The Mayor of Casterbridge*, Macmillan Master Guides, 1987
    There is good coverage of the early reviews of *The Mayor of Casterbridge* in the final section, 'Critical Appraisals'

Martin-Seymour Smith, *Hardy*, Bloomsbury, 1994

A detailed and very readable biography, which includes an interesting analysis of *The Mayor of Casterbridge* and Hardy's reactions to some of the reviews

LATER VIEWS

Hardy has been better served by twentieth-century critics, who have found much to praise in this novel. It is now recognised as one of the author's great tragic novels, and has been a favourite for many, including Virginia Woolf. There have been a number of reappraisals of Hardy and he has been claimed as the last great Victorian novelist, a **modernist**, a writer of nostalgic **pastoral** fiction and as a social commentator who presents radical ideas about men and women.

One school of thought focuses on Hardy's presumed regret at the decline in old rural ways. Critics who adopt this point of view suggest that Hardy laments the decline of traditional farming methods and regrets the scientific, commercial approach that displaced them; thus Farfrae is the 'villain' in *The Mayor of Casterbridge*. Douglas Brown argues that Hardy's great novels show the invasion and disturbance of the rural world by the new urban world. The Alien Invader (Farfrae) seeks to destroy Agricultural Man (Henchard). There can be no doubt that Hardy wishes us to sympathise with Henchard, but it is difficult to see the wayward mayor as an untouched and naïve countryman who is displaced by an alien invader. Henchard is a profiteer and he initially extends a warm welcome to Farfrae and benefits from his new methods, as the rest of Casterbridge does.

Other critics have focused on Hardy's pessimism, exploring the implications of his rejection of Providence. Many feel that what we see in the novels is an undisciplined universe, in which the social order is temporary and open to subversion. At times the natural world also appears to be malignant in *The Mayor of Casterbridge*. Frederick Karl has argued that Henchard is destroyed by the forces of a morally indifferent universe upon which he has presumed to impose his will. Others have suggested that Henchard's demise demonstrates that there are irrational forces at work in the world. It has also been argued that Henchard violates the moral order and is thus responsible for his own fate. A number of critics have commented on the different qualities in Henchard that bring about his downfall. Critics see Hardy's fictional portrayal of Fate, Destiny and Time as being central to his pessimistic philosophical outlook. Hardy, however, preferred to call himself a 'meliorist'; he believed that it was within man's power to make life better if he tried. There is a good deal of human sympathy in *The Mayor of Casterbridge*; even Henchard, who is frequently in thrall to his negative, destructive impulses, attempts to do good. There is another view which asserts that Hardy is seeking to examine the effects on character of heredity, environment and circumstances in his portrait of Henchard.

For Simon Gatrell, *The Mayor of Casterbridge* is about 'frustrated power'. Merryn Williams suggests that Hardy explores 'the Victorian Myth of "getting on"'. These attempts to define the novel's central theme suggest its contemporary relevance. Many critics have noted the overwhelming importance of the market place and business in *The Mayor of Casterbridge*, and commented on the class relations and social distinctions that dominate the book. John Peck says that the **protagonist** is 'torn between a sense of social duty and the force of his temperament'; instinctual man is pitted against the social order. Henchard is in an untenable position because his social ambition cannot override his nature, which forces him to rebel. At the same time, Williams suggests, Hardy shows us that the 'one thing that really matters is solidarity', although the novelist also 'stresses the only way to live in a community is not to ask much from it'.

Many critics have commented on how little romance there is in the book. It might also be argued that the relationships presented are hardly romantic. Virginia Woolf suggested that love is often 'a catastrophe' in Hardy's novels, and there is evidence to support this view in *The Mayor*; Henchard, Susan and Lucetta all suffer in their relationships. We see examples of mismatched couples (a typical feature of Hardy's fiction) and although Elizabeth and Farfrae are secure together, marriage is not presented as a perfect institution. In Hardy's work characters are often attracted to the wrong partner and lovers are the victims of passion and impulse; Henchard and Farfrae both fall prey to impulsive passion.

Douglas Brown, *Thomas Hardy*, Longman, 1961

> An influential study of Hardy which includes a chapter on *The Mayor of Casterbridge*. This chapter is also reproduced in the Macmillan Casebook referred to above

Simon Gatrell, *Thomas Hardy and the Proper Study of Mankind*, Macmillan, 1993

> Covers Hardy's major novels, and includes a persuasive appraisal of *The Mayor of Casterbridge*

Frederick Karl, 'The Mayor of Casterbridge: A New Fiction Defined', *Modern Fictional Studies*, VI (Autumn 1960), 195–213

Merryn Williams, *A Preface to Hardy*, Longman, 1976

> A very thorough study of Hardy's life and the historical and literary background to his work. There is a separate chapter on *The Mayor of Casterbridge*

CONTEMPORARY APPROACHES

In recent studies commentators have focused more closely on Hardy's portrayal of class relations and sexuality. A materialist critic might suggest that Henchard is in some ways an 'enemy' of the workfolk and the festivities we associate with them. At Weydon-Priors his egotism leads him to disrupt the celebratory nature of the fair; it is possible to suggest the auction places Henchard in a position of antagonism to the workforce, which is later demonstrated in his treatment of Whittle. However, the skimmington ride suggests that the workfolk are capable of asserting their own rights; it also provides a counterpoint to the theme of work, which dominates this novel. What we have is a clash between an egotistical and isolated businessman and the collectivity of the workfolk. Who wins? When Elizabeth-Jane marries Farfrae it seems that rational, serious and moral characters have triumphed. But these two are not enemies of the festival in the same way Henchard is; Farfrae is associated with a delightful dance early in the novel.

There are feminist readings of Hardy's works, with critics divided about whether or not the novelist is misogynistic in his portrayal of women. Little attention has been paid attention to the female characters in *The Mayor of Casterbridge*, but Elaine Showalter has suggested that

Henchard might be regarded as a 'New Man'. In her essay 'The Unmanning of the Mayor of Casterbridge' this critic argues that Hardy's work reveals 'a sense of an irreconcilable split between male and female values', but that the novelist 'understood the feminine self as the estranged and essential complement of the male self'. In *The Mayor* he gives us 'the fullest portrait of a man's inner life' in nineteenth-century literature. For Showalter the first scene 'dramatises the analysis of female subjugation as a function of capitalism'. Henchard then severs all bonds with the community of women, but is forced 'to confront the tragic inadequacy of his codes, the arid limits of patriarchal power'. For Showalter, paternity is 'the central subject' of the book. When he is publicly and privately unmanned, humbled by the furmity woman, Henchard is gradually made to realise that dominance and authority are merely 'façades'; this leads him to Elizabeth-Jane with whom he is 'humanly reborn'. Showalter sees the ending of the novel as proof that Elizabeth has won both 'a moral as well as a temporal victory'. Showalter feels that Hardy's acknowledgement and pursuit of 'the feminine spirit in his man of character' makes *The Mayor of Casterbridge* a daring book, which led directly to the creation of those great heroines of the 1890s, Tess and Sue Bridehead (*Jude the Obscure*).

Elaine Showalter, 'The Unmanning of The Mayor of Casterbridge', in Dale Kramer, ed., *Critical Appraisals of the Fiction of Thomas Hardy*, Macmillan, 1979

> As well as the Showalter's excellent essay there are two other essays that include interesting remarks about *The Mayor of Casterbridge*: 'Beginnings and Endings in Hardy's Major Fiction', by Daniel R. Schwarz and 'A Regional Approach to Hardy's Fiction' by W. J. Keith. Kramer's introduction is a helpful guide to critical approaches to Hardy

FURTHER READING

Penny Boumelha, *Thomas Hardy and Women: Sexual Ideology and Narrative Form,* The Harvester Press, 1982

> Although Boumelha does not focus on *The Mayor of Casterbridge*, the first chapter, 'Sexual Ideology and the "Nature" of Women 1880–1900' provides some useful historical background

Raymond Chapman, *The Language of Thomas Hardy*, Macmillan, 1990

Detailed and interesting study of Hardy's language; comments on novels too

Margaret Drabble, ed., *The Genius of Thomas Hardy*, Weidenfeld and Nicolson, 1976

Includes sections on Hardy's life and works, and chapters on Hardy's Wessex, Hardy and the natural world and Hardy's philosophy

Ian Gregor, *The Great Web: The Form of Hardy's Major Fiction*, Faber and Faber, 1974

This influential book includes chapters on each of Hardy's novels, and there is a persuasive study of *The Mayor of Casterbridge*, incorporating comments on the changes Hardy made to the first published edition of the novel

Rosemarie Morgan, *Women and Sexuality in the Novels of Thomas Hardy*, Routledge, 1988

Although there is not much specifically on *The Mayor of Casterbridge*, Morgan's comments about other novels are helpful when trying to arrive at a view of Hardy's attitudes towards women

John Peck, *How to Study a Hardy Novel*, Macmillan, 1987

Robert C. Schweik, 'Character and Fate in *The Mayor of Casterbridge*', reprinted in R. P. Draper, ed., *Hardy: The Tragic Novels*, Macmillan Casebook, 1983

J.I.M. Stewart, *Thomas Hardy: A Critical Biography*, Longman, 1971

There is a thoughtful chapter on *The Mayor of Casterbridge*, as well as an account of Hardy's life

Keith Wilson, ed. *The Mayor of Casterbridge*, Penguin Classics, 1997

Wilson's introduction to this edition of the novel is excellent. There is a helpful section on the history of the text and maps of Casterbridge and Hardy's Wessex

Events	Hardy's life	Literary world
		1798-1844 Heyday of British Romantic Movement
		1832 Death of Sir Walter Scott
1834 Union workhouses established; transportation to Australia of Tolpuddle martyrs		**1834** Harrison Ainsworth, *Rookwood*
1837 Accession of Queen Victoria		
1838 Formation of Anti-Corn Law League		
	1839 Thomas Hardy, mason, marries Jemima, cook	
	1840 Thomas Hardy, their son, born at Higher Bockhampton, Dorset	**1840** Birth of Emile Zola
		1844 William Barnes, *Poems of Rural Life in the Dorset Dialect*
1846 Repeal of Corn Laws		
1847 Railway comes to Dorchester		**1847** Emily Brontë, *Wuthering Heights*
	1848 Attends village school	**1848** Harrison Ainsworth, *The Lancashire Witches;* birth of Richard Jefferies
1849 Prince Albert passes through Dorchester en route for Weymouth		
		1850 Birth of Guy de Maupassant; death of Wordsworth; Nathaniel Hawthorne, *The Scarlet Letter*
1851 The Great Exhibition shows first reaping and threshing machines		
1854-6 Crimean War		
		1855 Death of Charlotte Brontë
	1856-62 Apprenticed to architect, John Hicks; witnesses public hanging of Martha Brown, Dorchester	

Events	Hardy's life	Literary world
1857 First Singer sewing machine; first concrete mixer		**1857** Gustave Flaubert, *Madame Bovary*
		1859 Charles Darwin, *On the Origin of Species*
		1860 George Eliot, *The Mill on the Floss;* Wilkie Collins, *The Woman in White*
1861 Beginning of American Civil War		**1861** Dickens, *Great Expectations;* Eliot, *Silas Marner*
	1862-7 Works in London as architect; begins to lose religious faith	
		1866 Dostoevsky, *Crime and Punishment*
	1867 Returns to Dorchester to work for Hicks; writes *The Poor Man and the Lady,* which later George Meredith will advise him not to publish	
	1869 Moves to Weymouth to work for architect Crickmay. Begins writing *Desperate Remedies*	**1869** Anthony Trollope, *He Knew He Was Right*
1870 Foster's Educational Act; elementary education for all; from hereon depopulation of Dorset countryside	**1870** Restoring St Juliot's Church, north Cornwall, Hardy meets his future wife, Emma Lavinia Gifford	
	1871 Publishes *Desperate Remedies*	**1871-2** George Eliot, *Middlemarch*
	1872 *A Pair of Blue Eyes; Under the Greenwood Tree*	
	1873 *Far from the Madding Crowd* serialised; his friend Horace Moule commits suicide	
1874-80 Disraeli Prime Minister	**1874** Marries Emma	

Events	Hardy's life	Literary world
1876 First carpet sweeper; first electric candle; first twine binder for farmers	**1876** Move to Sturminster Newton; *The Hand of Ethelberta*	
		1877 Henry James, *The American*
	1878 *The Return of the Native;* moves to London	**1878** Leo Tolstoy, *Anna Karenina*
	1880 *The Trumpet Major;* very ill for six months	**1880** Richard Jefferies, *Hodge and his Masters;* Maupassant, *Boule de Suif;* Dostoevsky, *The Brothers Karamazov*
1881 First hydro-electric power station	**1881** *A Laodicean;* takes house in Wimbourne Minster	**1881** Richard Jefferies, *Toilers of the Field*
	1882 *Two on a Tower;* visits Paris	
	1883 'The Dorsetshire Labourer'; moves to Dorchester	
1884 Foundation of Fabian Society		**1884** Richard Jefferies, *The Dewy Morn*
1885 Siege of Khartoum	**1885** Moves into newly built Max Gate, Dorchester	
1886 Six 'Jack the Ripper' murders, East London	**1886** *The Mayor of Casterbridge*	
	1887 *The Woodlanders;* tours Italy; in London meets Matthew Arnold and Robert Browning	**1887** Emile Zola, *La Terre* (Earth)
		1889 W.B. Yeats, *Crossways, The Wanderings of Oisin*
		1890 Frazer's *The Golden Bough;* Ibsen, *Hedda Gabbler*
1891 Education made free in England	**1891** *Tess of the d'Urbervilles; A Group of Noble Dames*	
	1892 His father dies; beginning of estrangement between Hardy and his wife	**1892** Oscar Wilde's *Salome* banned

Events	Hardy's life	Literary world
	1894 *Life's Little Ironies*	**1894** George Du Maurier, *Trilby*
	1896 *Jude the Obscure*	
	1897 *The Well-Beloved*	
	1898 Wessex Poems; by now he and Emma are living virtually separate lives	**1898** H.G. Wells, *The War of the Worlds*; G.B. Shaw, *Plays Pleasant and Unpleasant*
1899-1902 Boer War		
1902 Edwardian era begins	**1902** *Poems of the Past and Present*	**1902** Arnold Bennett, *Anna of the Five Towns*; William James, *Varieties of Religious Experience*; Joseph Conrad, 'Heart of Darkness'
	1904 *The Dynasts (Part 1)*; his mother dies	
	1906 & 8 Remainder of *The Dynasts* published	**1908** E.M. Forster, *Room with a View*
1910 Accession of George V	**1910** *Time's Laughing-Stocks*	
	1911 Awarded Order of Merit	**1911** Edith Wharton, *Ethan Frome*; Ezra Pound, *Canzone*
	1912 Emma dies suddenly	
	1913 *A Changed Man and Other Tales*	
1914-18 First World War	**1914** Marries Florence Emily Dugdale, his secretary; *Satires of Circumstance*	
	1917 *Moments of Vision*	
	1922 *Late Lyrics and Earlier*	
	1923 *The Famous Tragedy of the Queen of Cornwall*	
		1925 F. Scott Fitzgerald, *The Great Gatsby*
	1928 Death of Thomas Hardy; his ashes buried in Poets' Corner — his heart at Stinsford	**1928** Aldous Huxley, *Point Counterpoint*

alliteration a sequence of repeated consonantal sounds in a stretch of language, usually at the beginning of words or stressed syllables

closure the impression of completeness and finality achieved by the ending of some literary works

epilogue concluding speech or passage in a work of literature, often summing up and commenting on what has gone before

feminist feminism is, broadly speaking, a political movement claiming political and economic equality of women with men. Feminist criticism and scholarship seek to explore or expose the masculine 'bias' in texts and challenge traditional ideas about them, constructing and then offering a feminine perspective on works of art. Since the late 1960s feminist theories about literature and language, and feminist interpretations of texts have multiplied enormously. Feminism has its roots in previous centuries; early texts championing women's rights include Mary Wollstonecraft's *A Vindication of the Rights of Women* (1792) and J. S. Mill's *The Subjection of Women* (1869)

flashback narrative technique used to introduce a past event or memory that is significant to the plot, it disrupts the time sequence of the work

foreshadowing technique used to hint at or prepare the reader for later events or a turning point in a work of literature

imagery word-picture, description of some visible scene or object, figurative language in a piece of literature (metaphors and similes); or all the words which refer to objects and qualities which appeal to the senses and feelings

irony saying one thing while you mean another. However, not all ironical statements in literature are as easily discerned or understood; in certain cases the context will make clear the true meaning intended, but sometimes the writer will have to rely on the reader sharing values and knowledge in order for his or her meaning to be understood. Ironic literature characteristically presents a variety of possible points of view about its subject matter. Irony might also indicate the incongruity between what is expected and what actually occurs. In Hardy's novels ill-timed events or arrivals are ironic

materialist criticism that considers literature in relation to its capacity to reflect the struggle between the classes, and the economic conditions that lie at the basis of man's intellectual and social evolution

melodramatic any kind of writing that relies on sensational happenings, violent action and improbable events. Originally melodrama meant a play with music, including early opera; later melodrama became a minor genre in the nineteenth century

metaphor goes further than a comparison between two different things or ideas by fusing them together: one thing is described as being another thing, thus 'carrying over' all its associations.

modernist 'Modernism' is the label that distinguishes some characteristics of twentieth-century writing, in so far as it differs from the literary conventions inherited from the nineteenth century. The most typical 'modernist' feature of twentieth-century literature is its experimental quality, which is thought to be a response to living in the 'modern' world, that is to say, one characterised by scientific, industrial and technical change. Modernist writers throw old formal conventions away and reject traditional subjects, often experimenting with form and content

naturalism a brand of realism, naturalism expresses a post-Darwinian view of life in which man is seen as fundamentally no more than a specialised animal, subject wholly to natural forces such as heredity and environment. Man's spiritual or intellectual aspirations are seen as meaningless. Typical subject matter is the miserable and poverty-stricken, or those driven by animal appetites such as hunger and sexuality. Life is seen as a squalid and meaningless tragedy

omniscient narrator a storyteller with total, godlike knowledge of the characters and their actions

pastoral describes an imaginary world of simple, idealised rural life. Pastorals usually deal with a perfect, mythical world, set far back in time, a Golden Age of uncorrupted rural simplicity

pathos moments in works of art which evoke strong feelings of pity are said to have this quality

personification a variety of figurative or metaphorical language in which things or ideas are treated as if they were human beings, with attributes and feelings

prologue introductory section of a work

protagonist leading character in a novel or play

realism a general drift in the focus of literature, rather than a coherent literary movement. Many writers in the mid nineteenth century, especially novelists such as George Eliot and Balzac, saw themselves as confronting, describing and documenting new truths about people in society. Realist novelists attempt to portray ordinary life and everyday existence

simile a species of metaphorical writing in which one thing is said to be like another. Similes always contain the words 'like' or 'as'

symbol something that represents something else (often an idea or quality) by analogy or association

verisimilitude the property in a work of literature resembling the 'truth' in its depiction of the appearance of things. An attribute of realism. Verisimilitude depends not on any direct relationship with 'reality', but more on a collection of literary conventions, consisting of the choice of certain kinds of materials and approach, and the avoidance of obvious improbabilities; the aim is to give the appearance of 'reality'

AUTHOR OF THIS NOTE

Rebecca Warren works in Further Education, teaching English Language and Literature. She was educated at the Universities of Stirling, California (Berkeley), Warwick and Leicester. She is the author of the York Notes on *King Lear* and *Othello*.

York Notes Advanced (£3.99 each)

Margaret Atwood
The Handmaid's Tale

Jane Austen
Mansfield Park

Jane Austen
Persuasion

Jane Austen
Pride and Prejudice

Alan Bennett
Talking Heads

William Blake
Songs of Innocence and of Experience

Charlotte Brontë
Jane Eyre

Emily Brontë
Wuthering Heights

Geoffrey Chaucer
The Franklin's Tale

Geoffrey Chaucer
General Prologue to the Canterbury Tales

Geoffrey Chaucer
The Wife of Bath's Prologue and Tale

Joseph Conrad
Heart of Darkness

Charles Dickens
Great Expectations

John Donne
Selected Poems

George Eliot
The Mill on the Floss

F. Scott Fitzgerald
The Great Gatsby

E.M. Forster
A Passage to India

Brian Friel
Translations

Thomas Hardy
The Mayor of Casterbridge

Thomas Hardy
Tess of the d'Urbervilles

Seamus Heaney
Selected Poems from Opened Ground

Nathaniel Hawthorne
The Scarlet Letter

James Joyce
Dubliners

John Keats
Selected Poems

Christopher Marlowe
Doctor Faustus

Arthur Miller
Death of a Salesman

Toni Morrison
Beloved

William Shakespeare
Antony and Cleopatra

William Shakespeare
As You Like It

William Shakespeare
Hamlet

William Shakespeare
King Lear

William Shakespeare
Measure for Measure

William Shakespeare
The Merchant of Venice

William Shakespeare
Much Ado About Nothing

William Shakespeare
Othello

William Shakespeare
Romeo and Juliet

William Shakespeare
The Tempest

William Shakespeare
The Winter's Tale

Mary Shelley
Frankenstein

Alice Walker
The Color Purple

Oscar Wilde
The Importance of Being Earnest

Tennessee Williams
A Streetcar Named Desire

John Webster
The Duchess of Malfi

W.B. Yeats
Selected Poems